THE SOLITUDES

THE SOLITUDES

OF LUIS DE GÓNGORA

The Spanish text with an English translation by

GILBERT F. CUNNINGHAM

Preface by

A. A. PARKER

Introduction by

ELIAS L. RIVERS

THE JOHNS HOPKINS PRESS

Baltimore

PREFACE *by A. A. Parker**

This translation of the *Soledades* of Góngora was privately printed by the author in 1964, in an edition limited to 500 copies, for distribution in the first place to his friends at Christmas. It was sent at my request to Professor Elias Rivers who, recognizing its great merit, asked the author for permission to submit it to The Johns Hopkins Press, commissioning from him at the same time a translation of the *Sueño* by Sor Juana Inés de la Cruz. The suggestion that he should translate the *Soledades* had originally been made to Dr. Cunningham by the Edinburgh University Press, but on my appointment to Edinburgh in 1963, I advised that its publication be postponed for the time being in order to publish first a translation of the *Polifemo* of Góngora, which I asked Dr. Cunningham to undertake. The interest of The Johns Hopkins Press means that the *Soledades*, instead of being published after the *Polifemo*, can be published simultaneously with it in Baltimore and Edinburgh respectively. In the event Dr. Cunningham did not live to see their publication or the completion of Sor Juana's *Sueño*. He died on August 25, 1967. The Preface to this volume thus becomes a tribute to his memory.

Gilbert Farm Cunningham was born in 1900 at Alva, Clackmannanshire, Scotland. His father had

*Professor of Hispanic Studies, the University of Edinburgh.

founded in 1889 a printing firm in that small country town. This subsequently became Robert Cunningham and Sons, Ltd., when Dr. Cunningham and his brother joined it. Under him as Chairman and Managing Director it rose to the position of one of the leading firms of quality printers in Scotland. Shortly before his death it merged with the firm of R. and R. Clark of Edinburgh.

Dr. Cunningham laid the foundation of his abiding interest in literature at University College, London, where he graduated with a B.A. degree in English and where, as he was proud to recall, he was taught by W. P. Ker. His interests centered in the art of translating poetry, which he pursued with remarkable versatility as a relaxation from his professional work as a printer. His first and always his principal love was Italian, but he translated also from Latin, French, German, and Russian, turning last of all to Spanish near the end of his life. In 1954 he was awarded the degree of Ph.D by Edinburgh University for a thesis on the English translations of Dante's *Divina Commedia*. This was subsequently expanded into *The Divine Comedy in English: A Critical Bibliography*, Volume I covering 1782–1900 and Volume II 1901–66 (Edinburgh, 1965 and 1966). His verse translations not privately printed include *Translations from Goethe* (Edinburgh, 1949); *Poems by Eduard Mörike* (London, 1959), with some translations by Norah K. Cruikshank; and *Jean de Sponde, Poems of Love and Death* (Edinburgh, 1964).

Despite this activity as a translator Dr. Cunningham was not a linguist in the ordinary sense of the word. He could not really speak or write well, much less pronounce, any of the six languages which he translated.

Yet he had an instinct for languages, seen in his extraordinary flair for grasping, seemingly intuitively, the meaning of any passage of verse in these six. Góngora is very far from being an easy poet to construe, yet though Cunningham thanked me for "elucidating some of the less perspicuous passages," the occasions when he needed assistance of this kind were not more than half a dozen—and he had had no previous formal instruction in Spanish.

His translation of *Polifemo* is the first volume in the Edinburgh Bilingual Library of European Literature which the University Press is launching and to which it was planned that he should make further contributions in the near future. This volume will contain a Memoir of him as well as a bibliography of his verse translations.

The Translator's Note here printed comprises part of the Introduction that Dr. Cunningham wrote for his privately printed edition. For this new edition an Introduction has been written by Professor Elias Rivers. Our thanks are due to Mr. Robert Scott, of R. and R. Clark, for help in the preparation of this volume.

TRANSLATOR'S NOTE

The translation of poetry is, of course, a task fore-doomed to at least partial failure. In the case of verse of such complexity and density as Góngora's *Solitudes*, it is impossible to do more than provide a clue to the excellencies that will be found in the original. The purpose of printing the Spanish text opposite the English is not to invite comparison, which is out of the question, but rather to give the reader the opportunity of referring to it for himself, and it is hoped that many will be induced to do so. I have used the same scheme of rhyme and line-length as the Spanish, and I have taken such liberties with the rhyming of English sounds as I feel a translator is entitled to do in order to secure a greater degree of flexibility. Many of Góngora's characteristic effects, such as his classical syntax, are impossible in an uninflected language like English. Others I have done my best to preserve. I have many times had to make the choice of evils which is the self-appointed ordeal of the translator, and I have many times felt dissatisfied with the results. I trust, however, that this version of the *Soledades* may do something to make Góngora better known to English readers.

It is a pleasure and privilege to conclude by making certain acknowledgments. This translation owes its very existence to the friendship and encouragement of Professor A. J. Steele of Edinburgh, to whom I am most sincerely grateful, not only for the help and counsel which he is well qualified to give, but also for his kindly sympathy which has meant a great deal to me in this and other enterprises.

I am most grateful to Professor A. A. Parker who, during the short time he has occupied the chair of Spanish in the University of Edinburgh, has found leisure to give me practical help in elucidating some of the less perspicuous passages, as well as saving me from some of the traps into which the unwary translator is all too prone to fall.

Few English-speaking students of Góngora can avoid acknowledging a debt to Professor E. M. Wilson, of Cambridge, that doyen of Hispanic studies, to whose English translation of the *Solitudes* many, like myself, owe their first knowledge of the poem. This pioneer version, published in 1931, has long been out of print.* It is made on a slightly different principle from mine, for though the form is the *silva*, Professor Wilson has, probably wisely, attained greater freedom by not tying himself to the precise metrical scheme of the original. Indeed, had this not been so, I do not think I would have attempted the task myself, but in the circumstances I have felt that a new rendering on a different basis was worth the endeavor.

No one can study Góngora today without being indebted to the work of the outstanding Spanish scholar Professor Dámaso Alonso. His various editions of the *Soledades* are indispensable, and have been of invaluable assistance to me. While I have not always followed his text or his interpretation, I have found that his commentary has again and again shed new light on the original, for which I am most grateful.

[*Edward M. Wilson's translation of the *Solitudes* was republished by the Cambridge University Press in 1965.]

The Spanish text printed here has been collated from several editions, with one or two amendments of my own. I have with some hesitation used the definitive version of lines 197–211 of the First Solitude, since this seems to be in accordance with the poet's own intention; but since the earlier form is so well known and has so much to recommend it, I have included it in an Appendix at the end of the text.

I should like to add my thanks to several members of my staff who have patiently carried out the work of typing and retyping successive drafts of the translation and thus helping to bring it to its final form.

G. F. C.

CONTENTS

INTRODUCTION *by Elias L. Rivers**

I

Góngora's poetic world is enigmatic at every level. Violently attacked and enthusiastically defended, he was the most controversial literary figure of seventeenth-century Spain. Even when viewed from the distant perspective of the modern literary historian and critic, Góngora's poetry poses fundamental problems of interpretation and evaluation. Should we consider his baroquely latinized, witty style to be the natural consequence of an evolution which began with the classical Renaissance style of Garcilaso de la Vega, dominant in the sixteenth century? Or was it, as his contemporary opponents maintained, the indecorous result of an eccentric literary heresy? The basic historical question of continuity and change becomes acutely paradoxical in the case of Luis de Góngora. He personally forged a new and highly original style, yet he was in constant contact with the classical tradition. For most of his latinate lines precedents can be found in Ovid or Virgil, Horace or Petrarch, Garcilaso or Herrera. But the contorted poetic density of the total result is unlike anything classical. By French neoclassical standards, Góngora's poetry, like Calderón's, clearly had to be condemned as a baroque excrescence of Hispanic barbarity. Schlegel and Shelley were able to vindicate Calderón's dramas, but it was not until the twentieth

*Professor of Spanish, The Johns Hopkins University.

xv

century that poetic taste was ready for a revival of
Góngora. Rubén Darío's "modernism" prepared the
way in the Hispanic world for the critical re-evalu-
ation carried out by Lorca's generation in Spain. In
1927, the tercentenary of Góngora's death, Don Luis
was acclaimed as master by an important group of
Spanish scholar-poets.

Góngora's poetry as a whole draws not only upon
the classical written tradition, stemming from Greece,
but also upon the popular oral tradition native to
Spain. His lyrical ballads and songs, belonging to the
latter, were unanimously appreciated by his own and
subsequent generations; in this he is akin to Lope de
Vega and to García Lorca. His satirical and burlesque
poetry perhaps bridges the gap between these two
traditions; he himself considered his burlesque ballad
on Pyramus and Thisbe to be one of his best works.
But the scandalous touchstones of the quintessential
Góngora have always been his *Polifemo* and his *Soledades*. Elaborately erudite editions with commentaries
and explications were published by seventeenth-century Spanish scholars, and these editions have been
very useful to modern explicators. Dámaso Alonso's
1927 edition of the *Soledades*, with explanatory para-
phrases, made this poem accessible to the Spanish-
speaking world. E. M. Wilson, of Cambridge, immediately began work on an English verse translation,
which was published in England in 1931. Since then,
ignorance of Góngora's poetry in the universities of
the English-speaking world may be attributed primar-
ily to the critical inertia of American Hispanism.

Not that the *Soledades* can ever be a popular work.
It is full of painstakingly enameled golden nightingales belonging to Yeats' Byzantium. Its raw material

is drawn from the bucolic world of nature; but the material objects of this world—the brooks, the trees, the chickens, and the maidens—have all been filtered through the sophisticated eyes and ears of a witty intellectual, who has elaborately wrought dense new verbal objects. Góngora apparently intended this ambitious poem to consist of four parts, but he completed only the first and most of the second. It is not clear what the total structure of the work would have been. The two parts which we have seem to be narrative eclogues belonging respectively to the pastoral and the piscatorial traditions; it has been suggested that the third would have dealt with forests and the fourth with deserts. The focal point of view is provided by the central character, a shipwrecked wanderer, through whose eyes we observe mountains, plains, villages, and seashore. He is a "pilgrim of love," an exile from the city, where he has suffered disillusion at the courtly hands of a cruel lady. In the country he finds that lovers are more fortunate in the natural fulfillment of their desires. Though the form is narrative, the tone is one of lyrical meditation upon the glories of nature, profusely rich and varied, an almost chaotic realm of countless colors, sounds, and shapes, which resemble one another in many different ways. For Góngora, it is Art that must impose order and human meaning upon a material world. Great poetry, for him, must laboriously create, from verbal reflections of the fragments of this world, a new and highly artificial world which is dense not only with natural materials but also with cultural materials of every sort. Góngora, using all the literary devices and allusions of Antiquity and the Renaissance, freely plunders a soulless *natura naturata* in search of those bits and pieces which are needed to give new life and texture to the worn commonplaces of the classical tradition. Or, we might equally well say, he uses a narrative thread and the commonplaces of the tradition to give rational coherence to those brilliantly sensuous images and witty metaphors which are the lifeblood of his poetry. It is in this way that Góngora creates an authentically new poetry which is one of the great artistic achievements of the European Baroque.

In the *Soledades* Góngora explicitly emphasizes the primitivistic virtues of pastoral life. An old farmer's denunciation of overseas commerce is not only a Horatian commonplace but, as R. O. Jones has suggested, a critical commentary upon the contemporary Spanish economy, which had been badly shaken by the influx of precious metals from the Indies. When Góngora metaphorically substitutes gold for wheat, he clearly implies something as to the nature of true wealth. His exaltation of natural reality in the *Soledades* raises to the highest level of preciousness the everyday details of life among farmers, fishermen, and falconers. But the irony of the pastoral paradox is very strongly implied in this poem, which urges us explicitly to return to a primal life close to nature, a physical world free from the moral corruption of modern city life. For Góngora's own point of view is the quintessence of learned classical culture and sophistication, as deliberately "unnatural" a style as that of any poet who has ever written. The paradox is that Góngora gives us a new vision of the world of nature by creating enigmatic verbal artifacts which can be deciphered only by the humanistically educated, constantly alert intellectual. The *Soledades*, quite unlike Wordsworth's poetry, imply that only elaborate poetic diction and the most cultured intellectual Art can truly appreciate the intricate sensorial glories of Nature's world, which the blissfully ignorant peasant is not even aware of perceiving. Thus Art and Nature are first restricted to their most concrete, physical aspects and are then pushed to their antithetical extremes, extremes which meet and merge in Góngora's hyperaesthetic materialistic poetry itself.

II

The life of Don Luis de Góngora y Argote is not without intrinsic interest. He was born in Córdoba on July 11, 1561, the son of a noble couple, Don Francisco de Argote and Doña Leonor de Góngora. A precocious classicist at the local Jesuit school, he spent four years (1576–80) of gay student life at the University of Salamanca, leaving without a degree. In 1586 he took deacon's orders to inherit his maternal uncle's prebend as canon of Córdoba Cathedral. We know from his ironic reply to the bishop's accusations of frivolity, in 1588, that Góngora was inordinately fond of bullfights, popular music, gossip, and the theater. "If my poetry has not been as religious as it should be, my excuse is that I know little theology, so little, in fact, that I thought it better to be condemned for frivolity than for heresy."

In his native Andalusia it was inevitable that Góngora should come into contact with the predominantly illiterate, oral culture of the region, where the social arts of conversation, storytelling, recitation, song, and dance are still much more vitally alive than are the solitary reading and writing of texts composed for the literate minority. At the same time, Góngora himself did belong to that minority, within which the most intricate elaborations of verbal arabesques were deliberately constructed as a barrier to popular, oral intelligibility. Nowhere else in seventeenth-century Europe were the oral and the written styles so far removed from one another, and no Spanish poet was more completely at home in either style than was Góngora.

All evidence leads us to suppose that our canon had a deeper acquaintance with sex than with sentimentality. He was witty, hard-boiled on the surface, but nervous, hypersensitive. He traveled widely in Spain as the business representative of his cathedral chapter. In 1617 his ambitions led him to move to Madrid, where he was ordained priest and granted a royal chaplaincy. But his political maneuvers at Court thereafter were most unsuccessful. The need to maintain social appearances and his passion for gambling led him deeper and deeper into debt. His life became very difficult indeed. After suffering a stroke in 1625, he returned to Córdoba an invalid and died there on May 23, 1627.

Some of Góngora's poetry had appeared in print, in anthologies, before his death, but his reputation as a poet depended upon manuscript copies which circulated among the sophisticated minority. The first *Soledad* began to circulate thus in 1613, provoking the envious enmity of Quevedo and many others. Jáuregui wrote the first major attack on the *Soledades* about 1614, and with this a long and bitter feud began, a feud based no doubt less upon literary principles than upon personal and regional antagonisms.

Immediately after Góngora's death, printed editions of his works began to appear. The first editor was J. López de Vicuña (1627), and the second G. Hoces y Córdoba (1633). José Pellicer published learned commentaries on Góngora's works in 1630; a more elaborate series of commentaries is that of J. García de Salcedo Coronel (1636–45). These editions established Góngora's supremacy in Spanish poetry for the entire century. Dámaso Alonso's modern editions of the *Soledades* and the *Polifemo* have made them available once more to the Spanish-speaking world. Professor E. M. Wilson's 1931 version of the *Soledades*, republished in 1965 by the Cambridge University Press, accomplished something similar in England. The same press has also published an excellent introduction and selection, in Spanish, by Professor R. O. Jones, *Poems of Góngora* (1966).

THE SOLITUDES

DEDICATORIA
al Duque de Béjar

Pasos de un peregrino son errante
cuantos me dictó versos dulce musa:
    en soledad confusa
perdidos unos, otros inspirados.

¡Oh tú, que, de venablos impedido
– muros de abeto, almenas de diamante – ,
bates los montes, que, de nieve armados,
gigantes de cristal los teme el cielo;
donde el cuerno, del eco repetido,
fieras te expone, que – al teñido suelo,
muertas, pidiendo términos disformes –
espumoso coral le dan al Tormes!

Arrima a un fresno el fresno – cuyo acero,
sangre sudando, en tiempo hará breve
    purpurear la nieve –
y, en cuanto da el solícito montero
al duro robre, al pino levantado
– émulos vividores de las peñas –
    las formidables señas
del oso que aun besaba, atravesado,
la asta de tu luciente jabalina,
– o lo sagrado supla de la encina
lo augusto del dosel; o de la fuente
la alta cenefa, lo majestuoso
del sitial a tu deidad debido – ,

10

20

2

DEDICATION
to the Duke of Béjar

Such verses as my gentle Muse may grant
Are steps upon a wandering pilgrim's way;
    While some may go astray
In lonely mazes, others live inspired.

Encompassed by your javelins – these walls
Of pine, with battlements of adamant –
You scour the peaks, in snowy mail attired
Like crystal giants, filling heaven with dread;
While from their dens your echoing bugle calls
The beasts whose corpses stain your land with red,   10
Bursting its borders by their multitude,
And sprinkling coral froth on Tormes' flood.

Lean on an ash your ashen staff awhile,
From whose keen point ere long shall blood-drops flow
    Purple across the snow,
And let the busy huntsmen hoist their spoil
On some stout holm or lofty fir, which strive,
Though living, with the rocks for hardness; there
    Shall the prodigious bear,
Pierced by your shining spear, in death contrive   20
To kiss the pole that launched the fatal stroke.
Accept the holy shade of this huge oak
For canopy of state, or let a seat
Upon the spring's high bank replace the throne
More fitting to your godlike eminence.

3

¡oh Duque esclarecido!
templa en sus ondas tu fatiga ardiente,
y, entregados tus miembros al reposo
sobre el de grama césped no desnudo,
30   déjate un rato hallar del pie acertado
que sus errantes pasos ha votado
a la real cadena de tu escudo.

Honre suave, generoso nudo
libertad, de fortuna perseguida:
que, a tu piedad Euterpe agradecida,
su canoro dará dulce instrumento,
cuando la Fama no su trompa al viento.

Lord of all excellence,
These waters soothe fatigue and temper heat:
Stretched on the ample couch of this fair lawn,
To soft repose your wearied members yield,
And give that tuneful foot brief audience now   30
Whose wandering steps are by my pilgrim vow
Pledged to the royal chains that crown your shield.

May I, whom fortune scorned when free, now held
Within these generous fetters, honour find:
Euterpe, grateful for such grace, shall blaze
To her melodious lyre your well-earned praise,
Though Fame sound not her trumpet on the wind.

SOLEDAD PRIMERA

Era del año la estación florida
en que el mentido robador de Europa
– media luna las armas de su frente,
y el Sol todos los rayos de su pelo – ,
    luciente honor del cielo,
en campos de zafiro pace estrellas;
cuando el que ministrar podía la copa
a Júpiter mejor que el garzón de Ida,
– náufrago y desdeñado, sobre ausente –
lagrimosas de amor dulces querellas
    da al mar; que condolido,
    fué a las ondas, fué al viento
    el mísero gemido,
segundo de Arión dulce instrumento.

Del siempre en la montaña opuesto pino
    al enemigo Noto,
    piadoso miembro roto
– breve tabla – delfín no fué pequeño
al inconsiderado peregrino
que a una Libia de ondas su camino
    fió, y su vida a un leño.

Del océano pues antes sorbido,
    y luego vomitado
no lejos de un escollo coronado
de secos juncos, de calientes plumas,
    – alga todo y espumas –

10

20

FIRST SOLITUDE

In the sweet season decked with vernal flowers,
When the feigned bull that stole Europa's love
(Armed with the crescent moon upon his brow,
His hide resplendent in the solar beams),
*   The pride of heaven, seems*
Upon the stars in sapphire fields to graze,
A youth, as fit to bear the cup of Jove
As was the lovely boy from Ida's bowers,
Shipwrecked and crossed in love, lamenting now
The sweet and tearful strife of distant days,   10
*   Wept in the sea, and lo!*
*   The winds and waves were stirred*
*   By his complaint, as though*
Arion's dulcet lyre again they heard.

Torn from a mountain pine, with Auster's blast
*   Unendingly at war,*
*   A charitable spar*
Was dolphin yet enough to keep afloat
The unthinking pilgrim who had dared to trust
His pathway to the ocean's Libyan waste,   20
*   His life to a fragile boat.*

Sucked down to watery depths, then to the air
*   Spewed up again, beside*
A reef upon whose craggy head he spied
Cots of warm feathers twined with well-dried reed,
*   Still with salt spray and weed*

7

halló hospitalidad donde halló nido
  de Júpiter el ave.

  Besa la arena, y de la rota nave
30   aquella parte poca
que le expuso en la playa dió a la roca;
    que aun se dejan las peñas
lisonjear de agradecidas señas.

  Desnudo el joven, cuanto ya el vestido
    Océano ha bebido,
restituir le hace a las arenas;
    y al sol lo extiende luego,
    que, lamiéndolo apenas
su dulce lengua de templado fuego,
40 lento lo embiste, y con suave estilo
la menor onda chupa al menor hilo.

  No bien pues de su luz los horizontes
 – que hacían desigual, confusamente
montes de agua y piélagos de montes –
    desdorados los siente,
cuando – entregado el mísero extranjero
en lo que ya del mar redimió fiero –
entre espinas crepúsculos pisando,
riscos que aun igualara mal, volando,
50   veloz, intrépida ala,
menos cansado que confuso, escala.

    Vencida al fin la cumbre
   – del mar siempre sonante,
   de la muda campaña
árbitro igual e inexpugnable muro –,
   con pie ya más seguro
   declina al vacilante

Crusted, he found a sanctuary where
   Jove's bird had found a nest.

Kissing the sand, the plank that once had graced
   The broken ship, and floated   30
Him shorewards, to the rock he now devoted;
   For senseless stones still know
The flatteries that grateful gifts bestow.

The youth then stripped, and all that they had quaffed
   Of Neptune's humid draught
Back from his garments to the sand he wrung,
   Then spread them out to meet
   The sun, whose gentle tongue
Licked them with gradual and temperate heat
And mild insistence, till his kindly aid   40
Sucked the least moisture from the tiniest thread.

Soon as on the horizon's boundaries
(Whose line, now scarce distinguishable, turned
Waves into hills and mountains into seas)
   Sunset no longer burned,
The unhappy outcast, having donned again
The vesture rescued from the cruel main,
Trod down the twilight in the thorny shade
And, less exhausted than discomfited,
   Rocks that might well have daunted   50
The swiftest pinion's daring flight, he mounted.

   Scaling at length the height
   (Of soundless countryside
   And never silent sea
The mutual bound and daunting battlement),
   With firmer foot he went
   Downwards again and spied

breve esplendor de mal distinta lumbre:
farol de una cabaña
60   que sobre el ferro está, en aquel incierto
golfo de sombras anunciando el puerto.

«Rayos – les dice – ya que no de Leda
trémulos hijos, sed de mi fortuna
término luminoso.» Y – recelando
de invidiosa bárbara arboleda
    interposición, cuando
de vientos no conjuración alguna –
    cual, haciendo el villano
la fragosa montaña fácil llano,
70   atento sigue aquella
– aun a pesar de las tinieblas bella,
aun a pesar de las estrellas clara –
    piedra, indigna tiara
– si tradición apócrifa no miente –
de animal tenebroso, cuya frente
carro es brillante de nocturno día:
    tal, diligente, el paso
    el joven apresura,
    midiendo la espesura
80   con igual pie que el raso,
fijo – a despecho de la niebla fría –
en el carbunclo, norte de su aguja,
o el Austro brame o la arboleda cruja.

    El can ya, vigilante,
convoca, despidiendo al caminante;
    y la que desviada
luz poca pareció, tanta es vecina,
que yace en ella la robusta encina,
mariposa en cenizas desatada.

A sudden glint of dim and tremulous light:
　　A cottage lamp maybe –
An anchored beacon, piercing from afar　　　　　　　60
These shadowy gulfs, to mark the harbour bar.

'O rays, if not the mocking fire,' he cried,
'Of Leda's sons, in you my woes may find
A luminous conclusion!' Then afraid
The barbarous thicket might in envy hide
　　The beacon with its shade,
Even unassisted by the treacherous wind,
　　Just as the careful swain
Treads the rude mountain like a level plain,
　　Following the stone whose light　　　　　　70
Is beautiful, however dark the night,
Radiant, however clear the starry heaven,
　　Which, if belief be given
To dubious legend, crowns the unworthy head
Of a dark beast, whose temples, it is said,
Seem the bright chariot of a midnight sun –
　　So, pressing on, the youth
　　His eager paces plied,
　　Measuring with equal stride
　　The rugged and the smooth,　　　　　　80
Despite the chilling mist, intent upon
The carbuncle, the compass of his course,
While every bough creaked with the tempest's force.

　　The watchdog's hostile bay
Served but to guide the wanderer on his way,
　　And nearer as he came
What had before seemed like a spark now turned
To a wide hearth where a huge oak-tree burned,
As some great moth disintegrates in flame.

II

90   Llegó pues el mancebo, y saludado,
sin ambición, sin pompa de palabras,
de los conducidores fué de cabras,
que a Vulcano tenían coronado.

¡Oh bienaventurado
albergue a cualquier hora,
templo de Pales, alquería de Flora!
No moderno artificio
borró designios, bosquejó modelos,
al cóncavo ajustando de los cielos
100   el sublime edificio;
retamas sobre robre
tu fábrica son pobre,
do guarda, en vez de acero,
la inocencia al cabrero
más que el silbo al ganado.
¡Oh bienaventurado
albergue a cualquier hora!

No en ti la ambición mora
hidrópica de viento,
110   ni la que su alimento
el áspid es gitano;
no la que, en vulto comenzando humano,
acaba en mortal fiera,
esfinge bachillera,
que hace hoy a Narciso
ecos solicitar, desdeñar fuentes;
ni la que en salvas gasta impertinentes
la pólvora del tiempo más preciso:
ceremonia profana
120   que la sinceridad burla villana
sobre el corvo cayado.

A band of rustic goatherds rose to greet   90
The youth as he arrived, with homely ease
And simple words, like Vulcan's devotees
Ranged crown-wise round their central god of heat.

    O fortunate retreat
      At whatsoever hour –
A pastoral temple and a floral bower!
    No modern artist strove
With studied plan and elevated style
To match in grandeur with the lofty pile
      The arching vault above.   100
      Thatch upon oak instead
      A modest dwelling made,
    Which rural innocence
    Bars with a stronger fence
    Than sheep-pipe straying feet.
    O fortunate retreat
      At whatsoever hour!

    Here is no lust for power,
    No thirst for windy fame;
    No envy, to inflame   110
    Like Egypt's aspic race;
Nor she who, sphinx-like, wears a human face
    Above her bestial loins,
    Whose wily voice enjoins
    Narcissus' modern seed
To follow Echo, and despise the well;
Nor she whose insolent salvos now dispel
The powder treasured by a thriftier breed.
      Propped on his shepherd's crook
Rustic simplicity amused may look   120
      Upon the courtly cheat.

¡Oh bienaventurado
albergue a cualquier hora!

Tus umbrales ignora
la adulación, sirena
de reales palacios, cuya arena
besó ya tanto leño:
trofeos dulces de un canoro sueño.
No a la soberbia está aquí la mentira
130   dorándole los pies, en cuanto gira
la esfera de sus plumas,
ni de los rayos baja a las espumas
favor de cera alado.
¡Oh bienaventurado
albergue a cualquier hora!

No pues de aquella sierra – engendradora
más de fierezas que de cortesía –
la gente parecía
que hospedó al forastero
140   con pecho igual de aquel candor primero,
que, en las selvas contento,
tienda el fresno le dió, el robre alimento.

Limpio sayal, en vez de blanco lino,
cubrió el cuadrado pino;
y en boj, aunque rebelde, a quien el torno
forma elegante dió sin culto adorno,
leche que exprimir vió la alba aquel día
– mientras perdían con ella
los blancos lilios de su frente bella –,
150   gruesa le dan y fría,
impenetrable casi a la cuchara,
del sabio Alcimedón invención rara.

O fortunate retreat
At whatsoever hour!

From this umbraceous bower
Flattery's voice is banned,
Siren of royal courts, beneath whose sand
Many a vessel lies,
Relics of these delusive lullabies.
Here Falsehood does not gild the feet of Pride,
Though she display her feathery circle wide;   130
None hurtles seaward here
Whose wax-bound pinions carried him too near
Favour's deceptive heat.
O fortunate retreat
At whatsoever hour!

Not of these hills – fitter progenitor
Of savage beasts than men of courteous breed –
They seemed who now indeed
Welcomed their guest with grace
And candour, such as marked the primal race,   140
Long since within that wood
Content: their roof the ash, the oak their food.

Fair sackcloth decked, rather than linen fine,
The board of square-cut pine;
In bowls of box which, though recalcitrant,
The lathe had left simple but elegant,
They poured out milk, whose whiteness might have vied
With that of early dawn,
Under whose lilied forehead it was drawn,
Which, cold and thick, defied   150
The entry of the spoon, a witness still
To Alcimedon's rare mechanic skill.

El que de cabras fué dos veces ciento
esposo casi un lustro – cuyo diente
no perdonó a racimo aun en la frente
de Baco, cuanto más en su sarmiento
(triunfador siempre de celosas lides,
lo coronó el Amor; mas rival tierno,
breve de barba y duro no de cuerno,
160   redimió con su muerte tantas vides) –
    servido ya en cecina,
purpúreos hilos es de grana fina.

Sobre corchos después, más regalado
sueño le solicitan pieles blandas,
que al príncipe entre holandas,
púrpura tiria o milanés brocado.
No de humosos vinos agravado
es Sísifo en la cuesta, si en la cumbre
de ponderosa vana pesadumbre,
170   es, cuanto más despierto, más burlado.
De trompa militar no, o destemplado
son de cajas, fué el sueño interrumpido;
    de can sí, embravecido
    contra la seca hoja
que el viento repeló a alguna coscoja.

Durmió, y recuerda al fin, cuando las aves
– esquilas dulces de sonora pluma –
    señas dieron suaves
del alba al sol, que el pabellón de espuma
180   dejó, y en su carroza
rayó el verde obelisco de la choza.

Agradecido, pues, el peregrino,
deja el albergue y sale acompañado

He who these five years past had been the mate
Of ten score she-goats, whose sharp tooth had dared
To crop the grapes from Bacchus' brow, nor spared
The fruit of humbler vines an easier fate
(Love, in whose lists all others long he braved,
Crowned him, till rose a younger rival who,
Though softer-horned and shorter-bearded, slew
The champion, whence full many a vine was saved),   160
    Now furnished them to eat
The scarlet fibres of his tender meat.

Soft skins, draping the couch of cork below,
Now bring him sweeter slumbers than between
Brocaded sheets of costly damascene
With Tyrian purple dyed, a king can know.
No heady wine moves him in dreams to vie
With Sisyphus, pushing his painful load
Uphill, then, at the summit of the road,
Wake to the double mockery of a lie.   170
No trumpet shrills, no clattering drums reply,
To interrupt his sleep with warlike sound;
    Only the watchful hound
    Growls as he hears the breeze
Stirring dry oak-leaves on the neighbouring trees.

He slept, till at the song of birds he woke,
Whose bells of tuneful feathers, sweetly ringing,
    The news of morning broke,
And now the sun, from foam-decked pillows springing,
    Lit with his chariot's sheen   180
The humble cabin's obelisk of green.

The pilgrim, having thanked his hosts, was led
Out of the kindly shelter by his guide,

de quien lo lleva donde, levantado,
distante pocos pasos del camino,
imperioso mira la campaña
un escollo, apacible galería,
que festivo teatro fué algún día
de cuantos pisan faunos la montaña.

190 Llegó, y, a vista tanta
obedeciendo la dudosa planta,
inmóvil se quedó sobre un lentisco,
verde balcón del agradable risco.

Si mucho poco mapa le despliega,
mucho es más lo que, nieblas desatando,
confunde el sol y la distancia niega.
Muda la admiración, habla callando,
y, ciega, un río sigue, que – luciente
  de aquellos montes hijo –
200 con torcido discurso, aunque prolijo,
tiraniza los campos útilmente;
orladas sus orillas de frutales,
quiere la Copia que su cuerno sea
– si al animal armaron de Amaltea
  diáfanos cristales – ;
engazando edificios en su plata,
  de muros se corona,
rocas abraza, islas aprisiona,
de la alta gruta donde se desata
210 hasta los jaspes líquidos, adonde
su orgullo pierde y su memoria esconde.

«Aquéllas que los árboles apenas
dejan ser torres hoy – dijo el cabrero

And from the road a little way aside
They turned and mounted to a crag, whose head
Imperious towered above the plain's expanse;
A peaceful gallery now, but once the stage,
When faun and satyr in a bygone age
Peopled these hills, of revelry and dance.

 So wide a prospect stayed   190
His faltering feet, whose impulse he obeyed,
Motionless, where a mastic hedged with green
The lovely height, gazing across the scene.

Much as the little map he sees displays,
Still more, in cloud or sunshine ill-defined,
Is hid in distance or concealed by haze.
Wonder, though mute, in silence speaks; though blind,
Follows the shining stream, which had its birth
 Among these heights, whose course,
Tortuous at once and prolix, can enforce   200
Tyrannous abundance on the neighbouring earth.
A fringe of orchards on its banks is spread,
Which Plenty might have envied for its horn,
Could such transparent beads of spray adorn
 Fair Amalthea's head.
Houses are linked along its silver course,
 With prosperous dwellings crowned,
Embracing rocks and girding islands round,
From the high cave in which it had its source,
Till in the liquid jasper of the sea   210
*It sinks its pride and veils its memory.**

'Upon that pile, which foliage scarcely grants
The shape of towers today,' seeming to feel

*See Appendix, p. 145.

19

con muestras de dolor extraordinarias –
las estrellas nocturnas luminarias
    eran de sus almenas,
cuando el que ves sayal fué limpio acero.
Yacen ahora, y sus desnudas piedras
    visten piadosas yedras:
220   que a ruinas y a estragos,
sabe el tiempo hacer verdes halagos.»

Con gusto el joven y atención le oía,
cuando torrente de armas y de perros,
que si precipitados no los cerros,
las personas tras de un lobo traía,
tierno discurso y dulce compañía
    dejar hizo al serrano,
que – del sublime espacioso llano
al huésped al camino reduciendo –
230   al venatorio estruendo,
    pasos dando veloces,
número crece y multiplica voces.

Bajaba entre sí el joven admirando,
armado a Pan o semicapro a Marte,
en el pastor mentidos, que con arte
culto principio dió al discurso, cuando
rémora de sus pasos fué su oído,
    dulcemente impedido
de canoro instrumento, que pulsado
240   era de una serrana junto a un tronco,
sobre un arroyo, de quejarse ronco,
mudo sus ondas, cuando no enfrenado.

Otra con ella montaraz zagala
juntaba el cristal líquido al humano

A more than usual grief, the goatherd said,
'Stars, like nocturnal luminaries shed
    Light from its battlements,
When I, who now wear homespun, went in steel.
Round the bare stones of these dejected heaps
    Now pitying ivy creeps:
      Time, which heals every woe,   220
On ruins green endearments can bestow.'

Pleased and intent the youth was listening, when
A stream of dogs and weapons swept with force,
Steep as a mountain torrent's headlong course,
Bearing, behind a wolf, a numerous train,
Making the guide from his mild speech refrain;
    His pleasant escort ended,
From where the plain its stately view extended,
Showing the youth his road, he sped his pace
      Towards the clamorous chase,   230
      And ran with eager bound
To swell their ranks and multiply their sound.

Alone and marvelling the youth descended:
A warlike Pan and rustic Ares each
Belied the other in the shepherd's speech,
Whose opening eloquence so rudely ended.
Then, hindered by his ear, his feet were stayed
    And pleasantly delayed –
A mountain maiden plucked melodious strings
Under a tree, above a stream, whose hoarse   240
Complaint had ceased, as if the music's force
Hushed, though it could not check, the babbling springs.

Close by the first another maiden raised
The liquid to her human crystal, and

por el arcaduz bello de una mano
que al uno menosprecia, al otro iguala.

Del verde margen otra las mejores
rosas traslada y lilios al cabello,
o por lo matizado o por lo bello,
si aurora no con rayos, sol con flores.

Negras pizarras entre blancos dedos
ingeniosa hiere otra, que dudo
que aun los peñascos la escucharan quedos.
    Al son pues deste rudo
    sonoroso instrumento
    – lasciva el movimiento,
    mas los ojos honesta –
altera otra, bailando, la floresta.

    Tantas al fin el arroyuelo, y tantas
montañesas da el prado, que dirías
ser menos las que verdes hamadrías
    abortaron las plantas:
    inundación hermosa
que la montaña hizo populosa
    de sus aldeas todas
    a pastorales bodas.

    De una encina embebido
en lo cóncavo, el joven mantenía
la vista de hermosura, y el oído
    de métrica armonía.
    El sileno buscaba
de aquellas que la sierra dió bacantes
– ya que ninfas las niega ser errantes
    el hombro sin aljaba ;

250
260
270

She used the lovely channel of a hand
Which matched her features and the stream dispraised.

Each fairest rose and lily one transferred
From the green margin to adorn her head,
Whose beauty, mingled with the white and red,
Now radiant dawn, now flower-decked sun appeared. 250

In her white hands another with such skill
Clashed the black slates, the hearer might believe
The very rocks must listen and be still,
 And to this primitive
 But tuneful instrument,
 Sensuous but innocent,
  One moved with clear, straight glance,
And stirred the forest trees that watched her dance.

So many maidens by the brook were seen,
So many in the meadows could be told,   260
As must exceed all that the trees could hold
 Of hamadryads green.
 This beauteous flood increased,
From every hamlet round, the populace
 Of mountaineers, to grace
 A rustic wedding feast.

 A hollow oak stood near
And screened the youth, while on the beauteous train
He fed his eye, and with their rhythmic strain
 Regaled his listening ear.   270
 Bacchantes they might be,
But no Silenus in their ranks appears;
Nor are they wandering nymphs, whose shoulder wears
 No warlike armoury.

o si – del Termodonte
émulo el arroyuelo desatado
de aquel fragoso monte –
escuadrón de amazonas, desarmado,
tremola en sus riberas
280   pacíficas banderas.

Vulgo lascivo erraba
– al voto del mancebo,
el yugo de ambos sexos sacudido –
al tiempo que – de flores impedido
el que ya serenaba
la región de su frente rayo nuevo –
purpúrea terneruela, conducida
de su madre, no menos enramada,
entre albogues se ofrece, acompañada
290   de juventud florida.

Cuál dellos las pendientes sumas graves
de negras baja, de crestadas aves,
cuyo lascivo esposo vigilante
doméstico es del sol nuncio canoro,
y – de coral barbado – no de oro
ciñe, sino de púrpura, turbante.

Quién la cerviz oprime
con la manchada copia
de los cabritos más retozadores,
300   tan golosos, que gime
el que menos peinar puede las flores
de su guirnalda propia.

No el sitio, no, fragoso,
no el torcido taladro de la tierra,

Or could this streamlet, drawn
From sources in the trackless mountains, thus
   Rival the Thermodon,
With Amazons, disarmed and timorous,
    Now in a peaceful band
    Assembled on its strand?   280

   These in their merry play,
   The youth might well avow,
Must still from matrimony's yoke be free;
And now, crowned with a floral canopy
   Which almost hid the ray
Of new-grown horn that brightened on his brow,
A purpled heifer into sight was led
Beside her dam, no less adorned, among
A troop of hautboys, by a flower-decked throng
   Of youths accompanied.   290

One dangled in his hands a heavy weight
Of those same black and crested fowls whose mate,
The watchful herald of the sun, with bold
And tuneful note awakens every home,
Above his coral beard crowned with a comb
Of royal purple rather than of gold.

   Kids on his neck one bears,
   A speckled company,
Lively and sweet of tooth, each fain to feed
   Upon the flowers he wears   300
And he who finds he can the least succeed
   Whimpers despondently.

   Vainly the coney drills
His tortuous burrow in the roughest slope;

privilegió en la sierra
la paz del conejuelo temeroso;
trofeo ya su número es a un hombro,
si carga no y asombro.

Tú, ave peregrina,
310 arrogante esplendor – ya que no bello –
del último occidente:
penda el rugoso nácar de tu frente
sobre el crespo zafiro de tu cuello,
que Himeneo a sus mesas te destina.

Sobre dos hombros larga vara ostenta
en cien aves cien picos de rubíes,
tafiletes calzadas carmesíes,
emulación y afrenta
aun de los berberiscos,
320 en la inculta región de aquellos riscos.

Lo que lloró la aurora
– si es néctar lo que llora – ,
y, antes que el sol, enjuga
la abeja que madruga
a libar flores y a chupar cristales,
en celdas de oro líquido, en panales
la orza contenía
que un montañés traía.

No excedía la oreja
330 el pululante ramo
del ternezuelo gamo,
que mal llevar se deja,
y con razón: que el tálamo desdeña
la sombra aun de lisonja tan pequeña.

Vainly for peace they hope,
These timorous dwellers in the highest hills;
Their trophies now a huntsman's shoulder cumber,
Who boasts their lifeless number.

You, pilgrim bird, in whom
Ungainly shape and haughty splendour meet,   310
Born in the farthest west,
Hang, if you will, your wrinkled pearly crest
Against your sapphire-tufted throat to beat:
To grace a nuptial banquet is your doom.

Upon a rod across two shoulders borne
A hundred birds with beaks of ruby bright,
Shod as with crimson leather, come in sight,
Which well might put to scorn
The skins that Barbary boasts,
Though reared upon these rocky, barren coasts.   320

If nectar tears are shed
By dawn, as men have said,
Such drops, before the sun,
By early bees are won,
Sucking their crystal from the flowers, until
With cells of liquid gold the combs they fill,
Which now, in earthen jars,
Another shepherd bears.

His sprouting antlers still
Too short to reach the ear,   330
One led a gentle deer
That brooked the halter ill,
And rightly so, for Hymen disavows
The slightest shade of horn on married brows.

27

El arco del camino pues torcido,
– que habían con trabajo
por la fragosa cuerda del atajo
las gallardas serranas desmentido –
de la cansada juventud vencido,
340   – los fuertes hombros con las cargas graves,
        treguas hechas suaves –
sueño le ofrece a quien buscó descanso
el ya sañudo arroyo, ahora manso:
merced de la hermosura que ha hospedado,
efectos, si no, dulces, del concento
que, en las lucientes de marfil clavijas,
las duras cuerdas de las negras guijas
hicieron a su curso acelerado,
en cuanto a su furor perdonó el viento.

350   Menos en renunciar tardó la encina
        el extranjero errante,
que en reclinarse el menos fatigado
sobre la grana que se viste fina,
su bella amada, deponiendo amante
en las vestidas rosas su cuidado.

Saludólos a todos cortésmente,
        y – admirado no menos
de los serranos que correspondido –
las sombras solicita de unas peñas.
360   De lágrimas los tiernos ojos llenos,
reconociendo el mar en el vestido
– que beberse no pudo el Sol ardiente
las que siempre dará cerúleas señas – ,
        político serrano,
de canas grave, habló desta manera:

The winding road, which like a bow was bent
    (Whose curve, by following
The straighter pathway of the rougher string,
The fleeter maids had toiled to circumvent),
The wearied youths now conquered, well content
To make sweet truce between their shoulders broad   340
    And the unwieldy load.
The stream that lately brawled now softly flows,
Offering sleep to all who seek repose,
Thanks to its beauteous guests, if not indeed
To the sweet concert which their skill sustains,
Where the black pebbles' rustic harmonies
Clash from the ivory fingers' shining keys,
Bidding the streamlet run with silent speed
While yet the wind its furious blast restrains.

The wandering stranger left his nook before   350
    The shepherd who was least
Exhausted sought the ground and laid his head
Against the crimson dress his sweetheart wore,
To find repose for weary limbs and rest
His amorous yearnings on a rosy bed.

All these he greeted courteously, and they
    As kindly made reply,
Nor were the shepherds slower to admire;
Then, as he turned to seek the rocky shade,
One, who with tear-drops in his gentle eye   360
Observed the ocean in the youth's attire –
From which, despite the burning solar ray,
The sea's cerulean stain would never fade –
    Grey-haired and grave of face,
The stranger thus with prudent words addressed:

29

«¿Cuál tigre, la más fiera
que clima infamó hircano,
dió el primer alimento
al que – ya deste o de aquel mar – primero
370   surcó, labrador fiero,
el campo undoso en mal nacido pino,
      vaga Clicie del viento,
en telas hecho – antes que en flor – el lino?
Más armas introdujo este marino
monstruo, escamado de robustas hayas,
a las que tanto mar divide playas,
      que confusión y fuego
al frigio muro el otro leño griego.

Náutica industria investigó tal piedra,
380   que, cual abraza yedra
escollo, el metal ella fulminante
de que Marte se viste, y, lisonjera,
solicita el que más brilla diamante
en la nocturna capa de la esfera,
estrella a nuestro polo más vecina;
      y, con virtud no poca,
      distante la revoca,
      elevada la inclina
      ya de la aurora bella
390   al rosado balcón, ya a la que sella
      cerúlea tumba fría
      las cenizas del día.

En esta, pues, fiándose, atractiva,
del norte amante dura, alado roble,
no hay tormentoso cabo que no doble,
ni isla hoy a su vuelo fugitiva.

'What cruel tiger's breast,
　　Slander of Parthia's race,
　　Suckled of old the hind
Who first on any ocean dared to plough
　　With his ill-omened prow,　　　　　　　　370
Sinister husbandry, the watery dales?
　　Vague Clytia of the wind,
Trimmed not with petals but with canvas sails,
This wave-born monster, armed with heavy scales
Of beech, has long conveyed to many lands,
Once parted by the floods, more blades and brands
　　Than all the Grecian freight
Which other timber brought to Priam's gate.

That stone the sailor's industry soon found
　　Which, as the ivy binds　　　　　　　　380
The rock, attracts the boisterous metal donned
By warlike Ares, and with flattering eye
Ever observes the brightest diamond
Upon the nightly mantle of the sky
Nearest our northern pole; yet though it guide
　　Faithfully from afar,
　　When nearer to the star
　　Wavers from side to side,
　　Now to the roseate stair
Of rising day, now to the deathbed where　　390
　　Its ashes find a grave
　　Behind the cold blue wave.

Thus oak takes wings, relying on the force
Of this north-seeking lover's fixed intent,
Doubling the stormiest headland, confident
No fugitive island can escape its course.

31

Tifis el primer leño mal seguro
condujo, muchos luego Palinuro;
si bien por un mar ambos, que la tierra
400   estanque dejó hecho,
cuyo famoso estrecho
una y otra de Alcides llave cierra.

Piloto hoy la Codicia, no de errantes
árboles, mas de selvas inconstantes,
al padre de las aguas Océano
   – de cuya monarquía
   el sol, que cada día
nace en sus ondas y en sus ondas muere,
los términos saber todos no quiere –
410   dejó primero de su espuma cano,
   sin admitir segundo
en inculcar sus límites al mundo.

Abetos suyos tres aquel tridente
   violaron a Neptuno,
conculcado hasta allí de otro ninguno,
besando las que al sol el Occidente
le corre en lecho azul de aguas marinas,
   turquesadas cortinas.

A pesar luego de áspides volantes
420   – sombra del sol y tósigo del viento –
de caribes flechados, sus banderas
siempre gloriosas, siempre tremolantes,
rompieron los que armó de plumas ciento
lestrigones el istmo, aladas fieras:
el istmo que al Océano divide,
y – sierpe de cristal – juntar le impide
la cabeza, del Norte coronada,

First Argos, scarce seaworthy, Tiphys guided,
Then Palinurus o'er a fleet presided.
Both sailed one sea, now a mere pond, whose rocks
    Fence its whole circuit round,   400
      Save for the famous sound
Which with his double key Alcides locks.

Cupidity now steers across these floods
Not wandering trees, but migratory woods,
Leaving the hoary father of the sea
    (Of whose imperial sway
    The sun, which every day
Springs from his waves, and in his waves must die,
Sees not how far the utmost limits lie)
To toss the spindrift from his locks, while she   410
    Without a rival charts
The boundaries of earth's remotest parts.

And now three floating pines the trident wrest
    From Neptune's very hand,
Reaching a hitherto untrodden land,
To kiss the turquoise hangings which the West
Draws round the azure couch on which the sun
    Rests when the day is done.

Though flying asps from Caribbean bows
Poison the wind and hide the sun from view,   420
Cupidity, her conquering pennon tossed
On every wind, advancing, overthrows
Those beasts, fiercer than Lestrygonians, who,
Winged with a thousand shafts, people that coast:
That isthmus, whose dividing barriers break
Into two seas the Ocean's crystal snake,
So that its head, crowned with the Northern light,

33

con la que ilustra el Sur cola escamada
de antárticas estrellas.

430   Segundos leños dió a segundo polo
en nuevo mar, que le rindió no sólo
las blancas hijas de sus conchas bellas,
mas los que lograr bien no supo Midas
metales homicidas.

No le bastó después a este elemento
conducir orcas, alistar ballenas,
murarse de montañas espumosas,
infamar blanqueando sus arenas
con tantas del primer atrevimiento
440   señas – aun a los buitres lastimosas – ,
para con estas lastimosas señas
temeridades enfrenar segundas.

Tú, Codicia, tú, pues, de las profundas
estigias aguas torpe marinero,
cuantos abre sepulcros el mar fiero
a tus huesos, desdeñas.

El promontorio que Éolo sus rocas
candados hizo de otras nuevas grutas
para el Austro de alas nunca enjutas,
450   para el Cierzo espirante por cien bocas,
doblaste alegre, y tu obstinada entena
cabo le hizo de Esperanza Buena.

Tantos luego astronómicos presagios
frustrados, tanta náutica doctrina,
debajo de la zona aun más vecina
al sol, calmas vencidas y naufragios,

Joins not the tail, which the Antarctic night
    Studs with its starry scales.

Now to new seas beneath the southern skies   430
New galleons sail to gain a richer prize:
The snow-white daughters, born of lovely shells,
And those death-dealing metals, which so ill
    Rewarded Midas' skill.

Nor is it now sufficient that the sea
Lead out the grampus or recruit the whale,
Buttress itself with mountainsides of spray,
Deface its shingle with a whitened trail,
The signs of earlier audacity –
Pitiful even to the birds of prey –   440
Pitiful signs that strive to check in vain
The daring of the next adventurer.

And you, Cupidity, base mariner
Across these Stygian depths, the cruel waves,
Which for your bones open a thousand graves,
    Earn only your disdain.

That cape (within whose rocky caverns lie
New prisons for Aeolus' servants, where
Boreas, hundred-mouthed, raves through the air,
And Auster's dripping wing is never dry)   450
Your stubborn prow doubled with ready skill,
And by the words Good Hope men name it still.

Much that astrologers have prophesied
And sailors taught is now discredited;
Even where the sun is hottest overhead,
Dangers of calm and storm alike defied,

35

los reinos de la Aurora al fin besaste,
cuyos purpúreos senos perlas netas,
      cuyas minas secretas
460   hoy te guardan su más precioso engaste;
la aromática selva penetraste,
que al pájaro de Arabia – cuyo vuelo
      arco alado es del cielo,
      no corvo, mas tendido –
pira le erige, y le construye nido.

Zodíaco después fué cristalino
      a glorioso pino,
émulo vago del ardiente coche
      del Sol, este elemento,
470   que cuatro veces había sido ciento
dosel al día y tálamo a la noche,
cuando halló de fugitiva plata
la bisagra, aunque estrecha, abrazadora
de un océano y otro, siempre uno,
o las columnas bese o la escarlata,
      tapete de la aurora.
      Esta pues nave, ahora,
en el húmido templo de Neptuno
varada pende a la inmortal memoria
480   con nombre de Victoria.

De firmes islas no la inmóvil flota
en aquel mar del Alba te describo,
cuyo número – ya que no lascivo –
por lo bello, agradable y por lo vario
la dulce confusión hacer podía,
que en los blancos estanques del Eurota
la virginal desnuda montería,
haciendo escollos o de mármol pario

You kissed the kingdoms of the Dawn at last,
Whose purple lap the clearest pearls contains,
    And from whose secret veins
Comes precious ore to set their beauty fast.   460
Then to the aromatic woods you passed
Which, for the Arabian bird (whose track, though straight,
    Yet seems to emulate
    A rainbow in the sky),
First build a nest and then a pyre supply.

Next, water made the crystal zodiac
    Where, in its wandering track,
A glorious pine rivalled the burning flight
    Of Phoebus' axle-tree
And reached, after four hundred times the sea   470
Had made a dais for day, a bed for night,
The fugitive silver of the narrow strait,
The hinge that links two oceans, henceforth found
Ever and only one, whether their brine
Kiss Morning's crimson carpets, or the gate
    Hercules' pillars bound.
    And now, once more aground,
This vessel hangs in Neptune's dripping shrine,
Which holds in everlasting memory
    Its name of Victory.   480

Of anchored isles, a stationary fleet
In southern oceans, little need I say,
Whose numbers – though they wake not lust – display
Such charm, such beauty, such variety,
Stirring to soft bewilderment, as when
The limpid waters of Eurotas greet
The naked virgins of Diana's train,
Their lovely limbs like burnished ivory

o de terso marfil sus miembros bellos,
490   que pudo bien Acteón perderse en ellos.

El bosque dividido en islas pocas,
fragante productor de aquel aroma
– que, traducido mal por el Egito,
tarde le encomendó el Nilo a sus bocas,
y ellas más tarde a la gulosa Grecia – ,
clavo no, espuela sí del apetito
– que en cuanto conocelle tardó Roma
fué templado Catón, casta Lucrecia – ,
quédese, amigo, en tan inciertos mares,
500   donde con mi hacienda
del alma se quedó la mejor prenda,
cuya memoria es buitre de pesares.»

En suspiros con esto,
y en más anegó lágrimas el resto
de su discurso el montañés prolijo,
que el viento su caudal, el mar su hijo.

Consolallo pudiera el peregrino
con las de su edad corta historias largas,
si – vinculados todos a sus cargas,
510   cual próvidas hormigas a sus mieses –
no comenzaran ya los montañeses
a esconder con el número el camino,
y el cielo con el polvo. Enjugó el viejo
del tierno humor las venerables canas,
y levantando al forastero, dijo:

«Cabo me han hecho, hijo,
deste hermoso tercio de serranas;

Or cliffs of Parian marble – for whose sight
Actaeon well might hazard life and light.   490

That forest, spreading over many an isle,
Fragrant producer of the perfume brought
Across the desert with laborious speed,
Till from the mouths of the Egyptian Nile
Luxurious Greece received the sharp-toothed freight –
Not cloves, but spikes that spur the glutton's greed,
For Rome still boasted, when it knew them not,
Lucretia chaste and Cato temperate:
Leave them, my friend, where all my fortunes rest
        Beneath that treacherous sea,   500
With a still dearer pledge, whose memory
Feeds like a vulture on a father's breast.'

        The prolix shepherd sighed,
And many tears his further speech denied:
Such were the winds that once to ruin tossed
His wealth, the floods in which his son was lost.

Some comfort might the pilgrim have bestowed
With the long histories of his briefer years,
But now he saw the other mountaineers
(Still fettered by their burdens, like a train   510
Of patient ants, each laden with its grain)
Moving, and soon their numbers hid the road
As did their dust the sky; when, wiping now
The kindly tear-drops from his aged face,
The elder, rising, to the stranger said:

        'Son, it is mine to head
This regiment of mountain loveliness;

si tu neutralidad sufre consejo,
y no te fuerza obligación precisa,
520   la piedad que en mi alma ya te hospeda
hoy te convida al que nos guarda sueño
    política alameda,
verde muro de aquel lugar pequeño
que, a pesar de esos fresnos, se divisa;
sigue la femenil tropa conmigo:
verás curioso y honrarás testigo
el tálamo de nuestros labradores,
que de tu calidad señas mayores
me dan que del océano tus paños,
530   o razón falta donde sobran años.»

Mal pudo el extranjero, agradecido,
en tercio tal negar tal compañía
y en tan noble ocasión tal hospedaje.
Alegres pisan la que, si no era
de chopos calle y de álamos carrera,
el fresco de los céfiros ruido,
el denso de los árboles celaje,
en duda ponen cuál mayor hacía
guerra al calor o resistencia al día.

540   Coros tejiendo, voces alternando,
sigue la dulce escuadra montañesa
del perezoso arroyo el paso lento,
    en cuanto él hurta blando,
entre los olmos que robustos besa,
pedazos de cristal, que el movimiento
libra en la falda, en el coturno ella,
    de la coluna bella,
    ya que celosa basa,
dispensadora del cristal no escasa.

If such advice your leisure will allow,
And no express occasion hinders you,
The sympathy I bear you bids me keep   520
Your company, until the murmuring glade
    Invites to gentle sleep
Within that green-walled hamlet, which the shade
Of circling ash now scarcely hides from view.
Follow with me these maidens, and attest
Our country customs as an honoured guest,
Gracing our shepherds' wedding, for I see
In your attire more signs of quality
Than vestiges of shipwreck now remain,
Unless old age have much bemused my brain.'   530

Behind such beauteous ranks his path to tread
The grateful youth could scarce refuse, or slight
Such fair occasion's hospitality.
Gladly they went, for though the aspens made
No stately street, the poplars no arcade,
Fresh breezes murmured round them, overhead
Dense branches formed a cloudlike canopy,
Which strove like well-matched rivals, one to fight
The heat, the other to resist the light.

Weaving their voices in alternate song   540
Went the sweet mountain squadron, following
The tranquil current's course, which lazily
    Kissed as it flowed along
The sturdy elms, stealthily mirroring
Flashes of crystal, which the moving knee
Released between the skirt and buskin where
    It guards with jealous care
    The lovely column's base,
Yet gleams of crystal liberally displays.

550   Sirenas de los montes su concento,
a la que menos del sañudo viento
    pudiera antigua planta
temer ruina o recelar fracaso,
pasos hiciera dar el menor paso
    de su pie o su garganta.

Pintadas aves – cítaras de pluma –
coronaban la bárbara capilla,
mientras el arroyuelo para oílla
    hace de blanca espuma
560   tantas orejas cuantas guijas lava,
de donde es fuente a donde arroyo acaba.

Vencedores se arrogan los serranos
los consignados premios otro día,
ya al formidable salto, ya a la ardiente
lucha, ya a la carrera polvorosa.
El menos ágil, cuantos comarcanos
convoca el caso, él solo desafía,
consagrando los palios a su esposa,
    que a mucha fresca rosa
570   beber el sudor hace de su frente,
    mayor aún del que espera
en la lucha, en el salto, en la carrera.

Centro apacible un círculo espacioso
a más caminos que una estrella rayos,
hacía, bien de pobos, bien de alisos,
    donde la Primavera,
– calzada abriles y vestida mayos –
centellas saca de cristal undoso
a un pedernal orlado de narcisos,

Such was the mountain sirens' harmony   550
That even the most venerable tree
    Which from the raving blast
Least fears a ruinous collapse to meet,
Moved to the slightest movement of their feet
    And music as they passed.

Songbirds, like feathered lyres, in plumage gay
With painted hues, the rustic chorus crowned;
The streamlet too, eager to catch the sound,
    Changed its white flecks of spray
Into as many ears as, from its source   560
Down to its mouth, were pebbles in its course.

The shepherds proudly boast what victories
Their prowess in tomorrow's sports will bring;
The lofty leap, the strenuous wrestling-bout,
The dusty race on each its prize bestows.
Even the least agile boldly challenges
Neighbours and friends to meet him in the ring,
And all his trophies to his sweetheart vows,
    Who meanwhile from his brows
With rose-leaves wipes more moisture than, no doubt,   570
    Will ever steep his face
Next day in leap or wrestling match or race.

Alders and poplars fenced a spacious lawn,
Joining as many roads as stars have rays,
A place of peaceful concourse, where the Spring,
    Now shod in April's green
And clad in May's magnificence, displays
A sparkling shower of liquid crystal, drawn
From flinty rocks to which narcissi cling;

580   Este, pues, centro era
meta umbrosa al vaquero convecino,
y delicioso término al distante,
donde, aún cansado más que el caminante,
    concurría el camino.

Al concento se abaten cristalino
    sedientas las serranas,
cual simples codornices al reclamo
que les miente la voz, y verde cela,
entre la no espigada mies, la tela.
590   Músicas hojas viste el menor ramo
del álamo que peina verdes canas;
no céfiros en él, no ruiseñores
lisonjear pudieron breve rato
    al montañés, que – ingrato
al fresco, a la armonía y a las flores –
    del sitio pisa ameno
la fresca hierba, cual la arena ardiente
de la Libia, y a cuantas da la fuente
sierpes de aljófar, aún mayor veneno
600   que a las del Ponto, tímido, atribuye,
según el pie, según los labios huye.

Pasaron todos pues, y regulados
cual en los equinocios surcar vemos
los piélagos del aire libre algunas
    volantes no galeras,
    sino grullas veleras,
tal vez creciendo, tal menguando lunas
    sus distantes extremos,
caracteres tal vez formando alados
610   en el papel diáfano del cielo
    las plumas de su vuelo.

44

It made a shady screen   580
For neighbouring shepherds, and a loved retreat
For distant herdsmen, though the way was long
And often seemed as weary as the throng
    That trudged with weary feet.

Swiftly the thirsty maidens stoop to greet
    The crystal concert's snare,
As foolish quails hear the decoy that mocks
Their call, and hasten where beneath the green
Ungathered grain the net is spread unseen.
The poplars, combing green or greying locks,   590
On every twig melodious foliage wear;
Yet nightingales and zephyrs lack the power
To make the shepherd lads abate their pace;
    Unheedful of the grace
And harmony in woodland tree and flower,
    They cross the pleasant dell
And fragrant grass as though the pathway led
Through Libya's scorching sands, shunning in dread
The pearly snakes that rustle from the well
With foot and lips alike, as though the spring   600
Had worse than Pontine venom in its sting.

Onwards they went with undiminished pace,
Such as we see in autumn or in spring
Ploughing the boundless ocean of the air,
    Which are not ships that fly,
    But cranes that sail the sky,
Like moons that wax and wane, their outmost pair
    Closing and opening,
While letters with their flying quills they trace,
And on the sky's transparent parchment write   610
    The record of their flight.

Ellas en tanto en bóvedas de sombras,
   pintadas siempre al fresco,
cubren las que sidón telar turquesco
no ha sabido imitar verdes alfombras.

Apenas reclinaron la cabeza,
cuando, en número iguales y en belleza,
los márgenes matiza de las fuentes
segunda primavera de villanas,
620   que – parientas del novio aun más cercanas
que vecinos sus pueblos – de presentes
prevenidas, concurren a las bodas.

   Mezcladas hacen todas
teatro dulce – no de escena muda –
el apacible sitio: espacio breve
en que, a pesar del sol, cuajada nieve,
y nieve de colores mil vestida,
   la sombra vió florida
   en la hierba menuda.

630   Viendo, pues, que igualmente les quedaba
para el lugar a ellas de camino
lo que al sol para el lóbrego occidente,
cual de aves se caló turba canora
a robusto nogal que acequia lava
   en cercado vecino,
cuando a nuestros antípodas la Aurora
las rosas gozar deja de su frente:
tal sale aquella que sin alas vuela
hermosa escuadra con ligero paso,
640   haciéndole atalayas del ocaso
cuantos humeros cuenta la aldehuela.

Under the painted vaults of grateful shade
      The maidens lingered still
On carpets greener than, with all their skill,
The Turkish looms of Sidon ever made.

Before their weary heads had rested long,
As lovely and as numerous a throng
Of other maidens, like a second spring,
Coloured the borders of the crystal flood –
The bridegroom's kin, and nearer him by blood   620
Than were their homes more distant, carrying
Their gifts in honour of the bridal pair.

      A pleasant theatre
(And no mere dumb-show) with their glad accord
In this confined and peaceful scene they made;
And now, despite the sun, the flowery glade
Is white with snowdrifts, and upon the snow
      A thousand colours glow
      Across the tender sward.

Now equal time was left for them to gain   630
The resting-place they sought, and for the sun
To reach the darkening west, and as in flight
A tuneful flock of birds stoops to a bower
On sturdy walnut boughs, in some domain
      Where fruitful waters run,
When Dawn, in our antipodes, once more
With roses on her brow gladdens our sight;
So did the lovely ranks resume their way,
And, wingless as they were, their flight was swift,
While every village chimney seemed to lift   640
A smoking beacon to the dying day.

47

El lento escuadrón luego
alcanzan de serranos,
y – disolviendo allí la compañía –
al pueblo llegan con la luz que el día
cedió al sacro volcán de errante fuego,
a la torre, de luces coronada,
que el templo ilustra, y a los aires vanos
artificiosamente da exhalada
650   luminosas de pólvora saetas,
purpúreos no cometas.

Los fuegos, pues, el joven solemniza,
mientras el viejo tanta acusa tea
al de las bodas dios, no alguna sea
de nocturno Faetón carroza ardiente,
y miserablemente
campo amanezca estéril de ceniza
la que anocheció aldea.

De Alcides le llevó luego a las plantas,
660   que estaban, no muy lejos,
trenzándose el cabello verde a cuantas
da el fuego luces y el arroyo espejos.

Tanto garzón robusto,
tanta ofrecen los álamos zagala,
que abreviara el sol en una estrella,
por ver la menos bella,
cuantos saluda rayos el bengala,
del Ganges cisne adusto.

La gaita al baile solicita el gusto,
670   a la voz el salterio;
cruza el Trión más fijo el hemisferio,

Their fleetness put to shame
    The menfolk's slower pace;
And soon, their bands untied, all make their way
Into the village, while the sunset's ray
Yields to the spire that crowns the church with flame
And which, like some volcano's sacred peak,
Discharges wandering fires in empty space –
Fireworks, whose nitrous arrows leave a streak
Of brilliance, other than the lurid trail   650
    That marks a comet's tail.

The young man praises, but the elder blames
At Hymen's shrine so many torches lighted,
Lest, like the blazing car of some benighted
Phaëthon, one should plunge in ruin red,
    And that which went to bed
A village, wake, reduced by cruel flames
    To ashes, charred and blighted.

The senior led the youth to where close by
    Alcides' poplars stood   660
Combing green tresses, while the blazing sky
Lighted their mirror in the crystal flood.

    So many a maid and man
Lurk in the trees, the sun might well, to gaze
On the least comely, in a single star
    Compress his blazing car,
Which now on Ganges' banks greets with its rays
    The swarthy Indian swan.

The pipes and psaltery of rustic Pan
    To dance and song invite;   670
The steady Wain capers across the night,

y el tronco mayor danza en la ribera;
    el eco, voz ya entera,
no hay silencio a que pronto no responda;
fanal es del arroyo cada onda,
luz el reflejo, la agua vidriera.

Términos le da el sueño al regocijo,
mas al cansancio no: que el movimiento
verdugo de las fuerzas es prolijo.

680 Los fuegos – cuyas lenguas, ciento a ciento,
desmintieron la noche algunas horas,
cuyas luces, del sol competidoras,
fingieron día en la tiniebla oscura –
murieron, y en sí mismos sepultados,
sus miembros, en cenizas desatados,
piedras son de su misma sepultura.

Vence la noche al fin, y triunfa mudo
el silencio, aunque breve, del ruido:
    sólo gime ofendido
690 el sagrado laurel del hierro agudo;
deja de su esplendor, deja desnudo
de su frondosa pompa al verde aliso
    el golpe no remiso
    del villano membrudo;
    el que resistir pudo
al animoso Austro, al Euro ronco,
chopo gallardo – cuyo liso tronco
papel fué de pastores, aunque rudo –
a revelar secretos va a la aldea,
700 que impide Amor que aun otro chopo lea.

Estos árboles, pues, ve la mañana
mentir florestas, y emular viales

The sturdiest oak along the stream is stirred;
    Echo's full voice is heard,
Prompt at the slightest pause to make reply;
With watery panes lit from the glowing sky
In every wave a lantern has appeared.

Sleep puts an end at last to revelry,
But not to weariness – their movements tie
A hangman's noose to strangle energy.
The fires with many a hundred tongues deny   680
For hours to come the darkness of the night,
Like rivals of the sun, and with their light
Counterfeit day amid the shadowy gloom;
Then, as they die, their scattered members fall
In ash, contriving their own burial,
And make themselves a headstone for their tomb.

Night conquers in the end, and silence gains
Brief triumph over noise; though dolefully
    The sacred laurel tree,
Still bleeding from the axe's edge, complains;   690
Shorn of its pomp the alder now remains,
Shorn of its leaves which, severed by his hard
    And well-timed blows, reward
    The brawny peasant's pains;
    The poplar which sustains
The blasts of furious East and raving South
So bravely, on whose bark the shepherd youth
Finds makeshift paper for his lovesick strains,
Borne to the village, secrets now must tell
Which Love from other poplars kept so well.   700

Tomorrow in a counterfeit array
Of glades and avenues these branches will

cuantos muró de líquidos cristales
agricultura urbana.

Recordó al sol, no, de su espuma cana,
la dulce de las aves armonía,
sino los dos topacios que batía
– orientales aldabas – Himeneo.
    Del carro, pues, febeo
710   el luminoso tiro,
mordiendo oro, el eclíptico zafiro
pisar quería, cuando el populoso
    lugarillo, el serrano
con su huésped, que admira cortesano
– a pesar del estambre y de la seda –
    el que tapiz frondoso
tejió de verdes hojas la arboleda,
y los que por las calles espaciosas
    fabrican arcos, rosas:
720   oblicuos nuevos, pénsiles jardines,
de tantos como víolas jazmines.

Al galán novio el montañés presenta
su forastero; luego al venerable
padre de la que en sí bella se esconde
con ceño dulce, y, con silencio afable,
beldad parlera, gracia muda ostenta:
cual del rizado verde botón donde
abrevia su hermosura virgen rosa,
    las cisuras cairela
730   un color que la púrpura que cela
por brújula concede vergonzosa.

    Digna la juzga esposa
de un héroe, si no augusto, esclarecido,
el joven, al instante arrebatado

Be walled with liquid crystal by the skill
    Which country arts display.

To wake the sun out of the hoary spray
Needed not birds' sweet melodies at dawn;
Hymen himself had set his hand upon
The topaz knockers of the eastern bar.
        As Phoebus' burning car,
        Whose shining horses strained   710
Their golden bits in eagerness, regained
The blue ecliptic's track, the old man led
        His guest abroad to see
The bustling streets, admiring courteously,
No gorgeous tapestries of silken sheen,
        But leafy carpets spread
With forest boughs still decked in living green,
Arches across the spacious highways flung
        Where clustered roses clung,
And slanting plots and hanging gardens set   720
No less with jasmine than with violet.

The shepherd to the gallant groom his guest
Made known, then to the venerable sire
Of her who, quietly modest and demure,
In her own loveliness seemed to retire,
Yet by her beauty silent grace expressed.
So roses, while the crinkled buds immure
With green the glory of their virgin pride,
        Yet through the tiny gash
Between the leaves concede a modest flash   730
Of blushing crimson which they strive to hide.

        Fit for a hero's bride,
If not a monarch's, well the youth might say;
And then remembered, with a stab of pain,

a la que, naufragante y desterrado,
lo condenó a su olvido.

Este, pues, Sol que a olvido lo condena,
cenizas hizo las que su memoria
negras plumas vistió, que infelizmente
740   sordo engendran gusano, cuyo diente,
minador antes lento de su gloria,
inmortal arador fué de su pena.
Y en la sombra no más de la azucena,
que del clavel procura acompañada
imitar en la bella labradora
el templado color de la que adora,
víbora pisa tal el pensamiento,
que el alma, por los ojos desatada,
señas diera de su arrebatamiento,
750   si de zampoñas ciento
y de otros, aunque bárbaros, sonoros
instrumentos, no, en dos festivos coros,
vírgenes bellas, jóvenes lucidos,
    llegaran conducidos.

El numeroso al fin de labradores
    concurso impaciente
los novios saca: él, de años floreciente,
y de caudal más floreciente que ellos;
ella, la misma pompa de las flores,
760   la esfera misma de los rayos bellos.
    El lazo de ambos cuellos
entre un lascivo enjambre iba de amores
    Himeneo añudando,
mientras invocan su deidad la alterna
de zagalejas cándidas voz tierna
y de garzones este acento blando:

54

That he himself was, by a maid's disdain,
   A homeless castaway.

That Sun who doomed him once by her disdain
Burned the black plumes in which his mind was dressed
To ashes, but begot new misery –
The silent worm whose tooth remorselessly   740
Gnawed at his new-found happiness, and traced
Furrows upon his brow of endless pain;
For when in this fair peasant once again
A well-loved form he seemed to recognise,
Even in the shadow of the lovely face
Which lily and carnation joined to grace,
He trod in thought upon a snake, whose bite
Would have dissolved his soul into his eyes,
In outward witness to his heavy plight,
   But that there came to sight,   750
With many a stalwart youth and lovely maid,
Two festive choirs; a hundred tabors played,
With other rustic pipes, whose tuneful strain
   Accompanied the train.

The assembled shepherds now impatiently
   Summon the bride and groom:
His spring of life is at its fairest bloom,
And no less fairly blooms his worldly state;
The very glory of the flowers is she,
The very sphere whence lustres emanate.   760
   Then Hymen, having set,
Among these little love-gods' revelry,
   On either neck his yoke,
The maids with gentle voices and the men
With tuneful notes, in alternating strain,
The blessing of the wedding-god invoke.

55

CORO I

Ven, Himeneo, ven donde te espera
con ojos y sin alas un Cupido,
cuyo cabello intonso dulcemente
770   niega el vello que el vulto ha colorido:
el vello, flores de su primavera,
y rayos el cabello de su frente.
Niño amó la que adora adolescente,
villana Psiques, ninfa labradora
de la tostada Ceres. Esta, ahora,
en los inciertos de su edad segunda
crepúsculos, vincule tu coyunda
     a su ardiente deseo.
Ven, Himeneo, ven; ven, Himeneo.

CORO II

780   Ven, Himeneo, donde, entre arreboles
de honesto rosicler, previene el día
– aurora de sus ojos soberanos –
virgen tan bella, que hacer podría
tórrida la Noruega con dos soles,
y blanca la Etiopia con dos manos.
Claveles del abril, rubíes tempranos,
cuantos engasta el oro del cabello,
cuantas – del uno ya y del otro cuello
cadenas – la concordia engaza rosas,
790   de sus mejillas, siempre vergonzosas,
     purpúreo son trofeo.
Ven, Himeneo, ven; ven, Himeneo.

CORO I

Ven, Himeneo, y plumas no vulgares
al aire los hijuelos den alados

FIRST SEMICHORUS

Come, Hymen, come, for there awaits you here
A wingless Cupid, though he lacks not eyes;
The sweet profusion of his uncropped head
Upon his cheeks the down of youth denies –   770
This like the flowers that deck the early year,
That like the summer sun in glory shed.
A child he loved, and now in youth would wed
This village Psyche, peasant maiden born
Of sun-baked Ceres, in the twilit morn
Of faltering womanhood. Now join their hands
In the strong fetters of your nuptial bands,
    At his impassioned prayer.
Come, Hymen, come, and bless the bridal pair.

SECOND SEMICHORUS

Come, Hymen, come: a peerless virgin stands,   780
Herself of her own sovereign eyes the dawn,
Foretelling day through the translucent rose
Of morning clouds, so fair to look upon
That her two palms might bleach Egyptian sands,
And her two suns might warm Norwegian snows.
As many pinks as early spring bestows,
Like rubies set in gold, her hair to deck,
As many roses as from neck to neck
Their links in chains of concord interlace,
Are dingy spoils beside the modest grace   790
    Her blushing cheeks display.
Come, Hymen, come, and bless the bridal day.

FIRST SEMICHORUS

Come, Hymen, come, and with no common plumes,
Sons of the fairest nymphs our woods conceal,

de las que el bosque bellas ninfas cela;
de sus carcajes, éstos, argentados,
flechen mosquetas, nieven azahares;
vigilantes aquéllos, la aldehuela
rediman del que más o tardo vuela,
800   o infausto gime pájaro nocturno;
mudos coronen otros por su turno
el dulce lecho conyugal, en cuanto
lasciva abeja al virginal acanto
   néctar le chupa hibleo.
Ven, Himeneo, ven; ven, Himeneo.

     CORO II

Ven, Himeneo, y las volantes pías
que azules ojos con pestañas de oro
sus plumas son, conduzgan alta diosa,
gloria mayor del soberano coro.
810   Fíe tus nudos ella, que los días
disuelvan tarde en senectud dichosa;
y la que Juno es hoy a nuestra esposa,
casta Lucina – en lunas desiguales –
tantas veces repita sus umbrales,
que Níobe inmortal la admire el mundo,
no en blanco mármol, por su mal fecundo,
   escollo hoy de Leteo.
Ven, Himeneo, ven; ven, Himeneo.

     CORO I

Ven, Himeneo, y nuestra agricultura
820   de copia tal a estrellas deba amigas
progenie tan robusta, que su mano
toros dome, y de un rubio mar de espigas
inunde liberal la tierra dura;

Bid our winged Cupids take the air in flight.
Let some from silver-mounted quivers deal
A shower of musk, a snow of orange-blooms;
Let some beware lest any bird of night
On sluggish wing with baleful scream affright
The peaceful village while it lies asleep.   800
The nuptial couch let others mutely keep
Where, like the avid bee, the bridegroom sips
Hyblean nectar from her virgin lips,
    Rivalling acanthine red.
Come, Hymen, come, and bless the bridal bed.

SECOND SEMICHORUS

Come, Hymen, come, and borne by flying steeds,
Whose piebald plumage shines with azure eyes
And golden lashes, let the goddess ride,
Glory of all the choir above the skies,
Binding these knots, while year to year succeeds,   810
Till in serene old age they are untied.
Let her who now is Juno to the bride
Revisit oft, with changing moons, her home
In chaste Lucina's part, till she become
Renowned as some new Niobe, no rock
Whose pallid marble mourns her ill-starred stock
    In Lethe's dismal pond.
Come, Hymen, come, and bless the bridal bond.

FIRST SEMICHORUS

Come, Hymen, come, and bless both field and wood
With plenty, and let favouring stars give birth   820
To sturdy sons, whose stalwart arm subdues
The bull, and pours across the stubborn earth
Bountiful harvests in a tawny flood;

y al verde, joven, floreciente llano
blancas ovejas suyas hagan, cano,
en breves horas caducar la hierba;
oro le expriman líquido a Minerva,
y – los olmos casando con las vides –
mientras coronan pámpanos a Alcides
830   clava empuñe Lieo.
Ven, Himeneo, ven; ven, Himeneo.

CORO II

Ven, Himeneo, y tantas le dé a Pales
cuantas a Palas dulces prendas esta
apenas hija hoy, madre mañana.
De errantes lilios unas la floresta
cubran: corderos mil, que los cristales
vistan del río en breve undosa lana;
de Aracnes otras la arrogancia vana
modestas acusando en blancas telas,
840   no los hurtos de amor, no las cautelas
de Júpiter compulsen: que, aun en lino,
ni a la pluvia luciente de oro fino,
     ni al blanco cisne creo.
Ven, Himeneo, ven; ven, Himeneo.

El dulce alterno canto
a sus umbrales revocó felices
los novios, del vecino templo santo.
Del yugo aún no domadas las cervices,
novillos – breve término surcado –
850   restituyen así el pendiente arado
al que pajizo albergue los aguarda.

Llegaron todos pues, y, con gallarda
civil magnificencia, el suegro anciano,

Turns the young meadow's fresh and flowery hues
To hoar-frost with a thousand milk-white ewes,
Whose pasture in an hour lays bare the soil;
Crushes Minerva's trees for golden oil;
Weds with the vine the elm, till Hercules,
With grape-crowned branches, watches Bacchus seize
    The club that once he bore.   830
Come, Hymen, come and bless the bridal store.

SECOND SEMICHORUS

Come, Hymen, come; she, scarce a girl today,
Tomorrow as a mother may bestow
On Pales and on Pallas many a pledge;
Some in the glades shall wandering lilies sow –
A thousand lambs whose fleece, like crystal spray,
With tiny waves shall clothe the river's edge;
On fair white cloth Arachne's boastful rage
In gentle disapproval others prick,
But not portray how Jove, by theft or trick,   840
Glutted his lust, for, even on linen told,
Nor milk-white swan nor shining rain of gold
    Befit a modest brow.
Come, Hymen, come, and bless the bridal vow.

    The sweet alternate strain
Accompanied the newly wedded pair
Home from the neighbouring altar once again;
So oxen, scarce accustomed yet to bear
The yoke, after the first few furrows cut,
Soon make their way back to the straw-built hut   850
Which houses them, dragging the idle plough.

To all the guests, quickly assembled now,
Alike from mountain and from countryside,

cuantos la sierra dió, cuantos el llano
labradores convida
a la prolija rústica comida
que sin rumor previno en mesas grandes.

Ostente crespas blancas esculturas
artífice gentil de dobladuras
860   en los que damascó manteles Flandes,
mientras casero lino Ceres tanta
ofrece ahora, cuantos guardó el heno
dulces pomos, que al curso de Atalanta
fueran dorado freno.

Manjares que el veneno
y el apetito ignoran igualmente,
les sirvieron, y en oro, no, luciente,
confuso Baco, ni en bruñida plata
su néctar les desata,
870   sino en vidrio topacios carmesíes
y pálidos rubíes.

Sellar del fuego quiso regalado
los gulosos estómagos el rubio,
imitador suave de la cera,
quesillo – dulcemente apremiado
de rústica, vaquera,
blanca, hermosa mano, cuyas venas
la distinguieron de la leche apenas – ;
mas ni la encarcelada nuez esquiva,
880   ni el membrillo pudieran anudado,
si la sabrosa oliva
no serenara el bacanal diluvio.

Levantadas las mesas, al canoro
son de la ninfa un tiempo, ahora caña,

The venerable father of the bride
    With lavish courtesy
Extended country hospitality
On massive boards in seemly silence set.

On table damask let the Fleming ply
His subtle art of doubling, and thereby
The white relief of sculpture imitate;   860
Her homely linen Ceres here unrolled,
Laden with fruit, preserved in hay, so sweet,
The apples might have made a curb of gold
    For Atalanta's feet.

    Here none need fear to eat
Lest poison slay or drugs inflame the sense;
No burnished gold or silver cups dispense
The nectar of the vine, whose mingled sheen,
    In simple glasses seen,
Now burns like paler rubies, and now glows   870
    Like topaz tinged with rose.

Though first the fervent fumes of wine that preyed
On over-eager stomachs, yellow cheese,
Gentle as yielding wax, sought to allay –
The skilful hands with which the dairymaid
    Had pressed it from the whey
Were fair and white, and by the veins alone
Could from the milk that filled her pail be known –
It, like the elusive shell-imprisoned nut
And knotty quince, had failed, but for the aid   880
    The savoury olive brought,
Which once had calmed a greater flood than these.

The tables cleared, the Arcadian nymph, of old
Changed to a reed, supplied a tuneful strain,

63

seis de los montes, seis de la campaña,
– sus espaldas rayando el sutil oro
que negó al viento el nácar bien tejido –
terno de gracias bello, repetido
cuatro veces en doce labradoras,
890   entró bailando numerosamente;
y dulce musa entre ellas – si consiente
bárbaras el Parnaso moradoras –

«Vivid felices», dijo,
«largo curso de edad nunca prolijo;
y si prolijo, en nudos amorosos
    siempre vivid, esposos.
Venza no solo en su candor la nieve,
mas plata en su esplendor sea cardada
cuanto estambre vital Cloto os traslada
900   de la alta fatal rueca al huso breve.

Sean de la Fortuna
aplausos la respuesta
de vuestras granjerías.
A la reja importuna,
a la azada molesta
fecundo os rinda – en desiguales días –
    el campo agradecido
oro trillado y néctar exprimido.

Sus morados cantuesos, sus copadas
910   encinas la montaña contar antes
deje que vuestras cabras, siempre errantes,
que vuestras vacas, tarde o nunca herradas.

Corderillos os brote la ribera,
    que la hierba menuda

To which, six from the hills, six from the plain
(Their shoulders radiant with subtle gold
Which nacre fillets to the wind denied),
Twelve maids, whose numbers four times multiplied
The graces' lovely trio, entered now
In rhythmic dance, among them one who might   890
Be thought a Muse, did the Parnassian height
Such rustic dwellers on its slopes allow.

    'Live long and happily,'
She said, 'and age bring no monotony,
Save that the marriage knot shall bind you fast
    So long as life shall last.
Whiter than snow and bright as silver too
Be whatsoever length of vital thread
From Clotho's high and fatal wheel is led
To fill the scanty spool assigned to you.   900

    May all you undertake
    From Fortune soon receive
    A gracious answering smile;
    And though your ploughshare break,
    Your hoe and harrow grieve,
Yet in their season may the grateful soil
    Provide in rich excess
Gold for your flail and nectar for your press.

Sooner each tufted oak upon their slopes
The hills shall number, or each purple spine,   910
Than count your wandering goats or numerous kine,
Whose timely branding is beyond your hopes.

May lambs so many on your pastures roam
    As in their numbers seem

65

y las perlas exceda del rocío
    su número, y del río
la blanca espuma, cuantos la tijera
vellones les desnuda.

Tantos de breve fábrica, aunque ruda,
920 albergues vuestros las abejas moren,
y primaveras tantas os desfloren,
que – cual la Arabia madre ve de aromas
sacros troncos sudar fragantes gomas –
vuestros corchos por uno y otro poro
en dulce se desaten líquido oro.

Próspera, al fin, mas no espumosa tanto,
    vuestra fortuna sea,
que alimenten la invidia en nuestra aldea
áspides más que en la región del llanto.
930 Entre opulencias y necesidades,
medianías vinculen competentes
    a vuestros descendientes
– previniendo ambos daños – las edades.
Ilustren obeliscos las ciudades,
a los rayos de Júpiter expuesta
– aun más que a los de Febo – su corona,
cuando a la choza pastoral perdona
el cielo, fulminando la floresta.

Cisnes pues una y otra pluma, en esta
940 tranquilidad os halle labradora
    la postrimera hora:
cuya lámina cifre desengaños,
que en letras pocas lean muchos años.»

Del himno culto dió el último acento
fin mudo al baile, al tiempo que seguida

To match the blades of grass or pearls of dew;
*   And may their fleeces too*
Fall to your shears as freely as the foam
*   That flecks the brawling stream.*

Though rudely fashioned, let your shelters teem
With swarms of bees, who spread their busy wings   920
To rob the blossoms of successive springs.
As Araby, mother of perfumes, sees
Sweet balsam oozing from her sacred trees,
So may your hives exude through every pore
The liquid fragrance of the gold they store.

Be prosperous then, but let not fortune swell
*   With ostentatious speed,*
Lest poisonous serpents in our village breed
Jealousy more than in the depths of hell.
But between penury and opulence,   930
With prudent foresight shunning either ill,
*   May the years pass until*
They leave your heirs a modest competence.
Great cities, crowned with the magnificence
Of towers, have yet more cause to fear the strokes
Of Jove than those of Phoebus, for the skies
Will often spare the humble cot that lies
Beneath, yet tear apart the tallest oaks.

Like two swans, in the end, with silvery locks,
In quiet labour may you still be found   940
*   When your last hour shall sound,*
And, undeceived, let men your tombstone read
Where many years so short a record need.'

When the last accent of the solemn strain
In silence ends the dance, the bride is seen

67

la novia sale de villanas ciento
a la verde florida palizada,
cual nueva fénix en flamantes plumas
matutinos del sol rayos vestida,
950   de cuanta surca el aire acompañada
        monarquía canora;
y, vadeando nubes, las espumas
del rey corona de los otros ríos:
en cuya orilla el viento hereda ahora
        pequeños no vacíos
de funerales bárbaros trofeos
que el Egipto erigió a sus Ptolomeos.

Los árboles que el bosque habían fingido,
umbroso coliseo ya formando,
960   despejan el ejido,
        olímpica palestra
de valientes desnudos labradores.

Llegó la desposada apenas, cuando
        feroz ardiente muestra
hicieron dos robustos luchadores
de sus músculos, menos defendidos
del blanco lino que del vello obscuro.
Abrazáronse, pues, los dos, y luego
– humo anhelando el que no suda fuego –
970   de recíprocos nudos impedidos
cual duros olmos de implicantes vides,
yedra el uno es tenaz del otro muro.
Mañosos, al fin, hijos de la tierra,
        cuando fuertes no Alcides,
procuran derribarse, y, derribados,
cual pinos se levantan arraigados
en los profundos senos de la sierra.

Leading a hundred maidens in her train
To the arena decked with leaves and flowers,
Like some new phoenix, with her plumes aflame,
Dressed in the morning sunlight's dazzling sheen,
Attended by as many tuneful powers   950
    As plough the air's expanse,
Fording the clouds to set her diadem
Upon the king of rivers, by whose shore
Wide wastes are now the wind's inheritance,
    On which there stood before
Barbaric trophies of sepulchral woe
Built for Egyptian pharaohs long ago.

Trees that upon the common lately made
Counterfeit forests now no less supplied
    A coliseum's shade,   960
    A rustic wrestling-green
For valiant peasants who had stripped for fight.

Here, close on the arrival of the bride,
    Eager and fierce of mien,
Two stalwart wrestlers now exposed to sight
Muscles their linen garb availed to hide
Less than the hair which formed a swarthy pall.
Then they embraced, and if the sweat they broke
Were not of fire, at least they panted smoke,
Till, hindered by the mutual knots they tied,   970
Like vines that twist their stems round sturdy trees
One's ivy tendrils clutched the other's wall.
These cunning sons of earth, if not possessed
    Of strength like Hercules,
Yet, falling, from each fall contrived to rise
Strong as a pine whose firm foundation lies
Deep-rooted in its native mountain's breast.

69

Premio los honra igual. Y de otros cuatro
ciñe las sienes gloriosa rama,
980   con que se puso término a la lucha.

Las dos partes rayaba del teatro
el sol, cuando arrogante joven llama
    al expedido salto
la bárbara corona que le escucha.
Arras del animoso desafío
un pardo gabán fué en el verde suelo,
a quien se abaten ocho o diez soberbios
montañeses, cual suele de lo alto
calarse turba de invidiosas aves
990   a los ojos de Ascálafo, vestido
de perezosas plumas. Quién, de graves
piedras las duras manos impedido,
su agilidad pondera; quién sus nervios
desata estremeciéndose gallardo.

Besó la raya pues el pie desnudo
del suelto mozo, y con airoso vuelo
pisó del viento lo que del ejido
tres veces ocupar pudiera un dardo.

La admiración, vestida un mármol frío,
1000   apenas arquear las cejas pudo;
la emulación, calzada un duro hielo,
torpe se arraiga. Bien que impulso noble
de gloria, aunque villano, solicita
a un vaquero de aquellos montes, grueso,
    membrudo, fuerte roble,
que, ágil a pesar de lo robusto,
al aire se arrebata, violentando
lo grave tanto, que lo precipita

They share the prize, and then the victor's bay
To wreathe the brows of other four beside
Is granted, and the wrestling bouts conclude.   980

While yet two thirds of the arena lay
In sunlight, an audacious youth defied
        To meet him in the leap
The peasant circle who in hearing stood.
Prize of the sprightly contest, there was laid
A dusky cloak upon the verdant sod,
Which spurred some eight or ten bold mountaineers
To action, as at times in downward sweep
A flock of envious birds will fall upon
The owl, whose feathers move so sluggishly.   990
One clasps in each hard hand a heavy stone
As if to weigh his own agility;
One, as he loosens up his limbs, appears
To shake his body in a merry dance.

With naked foot the nimble youngster now
Kisses the mark, and treads in airy flight
Upon the wind such distance as might be
Thrice measured on the meadow with a lance.

Astonishment, in marble cold arrayed,
Had scarcely power to arch a wondering brow;   1000
Rivalry's foot, in icy rigour shod,
Froze to the ground. Yet noble impulse woke
One herd, though humble, to desire renown:
Bred in these hills, a stout and vigorous
        And mighty-membered oak,
Nimble despite his size, upon the air
He ventured, but he did his bulky mass
Such outrage that he soon was hurtled down

71

– Ícaro montañés – su mismo peso,
1010 de la menuda hierba el seno blando
piélago duro hecho a su ruina.

Si no tan corpulento, más adusto
serrano le sucede,
que iguala y aun excede
al ayuno leopardo,
al corcillo travieso, al muflón sardo
que de las rocas trepa a la marina
sin dejar ni aun pequeña
del pie ligero bipartida seña.
1020 Con más felicidad que el precedente,
pisó las huellas casi del primero
el adusto vaquero.
Pasos otro dió al aire, al suelo coces.

Y premiados graduadamente,
advocaron a sí toda la gente
– cierzos del llano y austros de la sierra –
mancebos tan veloces,
que cuando Ceres más dora la tierra,
y argenta el mar desde sus grutas hondas
1030 Neptuno, sin fatiga
su vago pie de pluma
surcar pudiera mieses, pisar ondas,
sin inclinar espiga,
sin violar espuma.

Dos veces eran diez, y dirigidos
a dos olmos que quieren, abrazados,
ser palios verdes, ser frondosas metas,
salen cual de torcidos

72

By his own weight, a highland Icarus,
Whom the soft bosom of the tender grass   1010
Made a hard sea for his discomfiture.

A shepherd of less bulk, but hardier,
    Following on the last,
    Equalled and even surpassed
    The hungry leopard's leap,
The nimble deer or wild Sardinian sheep
Who, deftly clambering from cliff to shore,
    Yet leaves no print for proof
Of where it set its fleet and cloven hoof.
With better luck the sinewy herdsman sped,   1020
As in the footsteps of the first he trod;
    Then one more kicked the sod
Likewise and made his journey through the air.

Each was rewarded as he merited,
And then the runners took the field instead
(Auster or Boreas these from mount or plain),
    So fleet of foot they were,
When Ceres gilds the harvest field with grain,
Or Neptune silvers, from his deepest caves,
    The ocean, lightly borne   1030
    On wing-like feet, might they
Have ploughed the crops and walked upon the waves,
    Leaving unbent the corn,
    And undisturbed the spray.

A score they are, following a track that goes
Towards two elms, which long to be embraced
Both as a leafy goal and verdant prize,
    Just as from bended bows

arcos, o nerviosos o acerados,
1040   con silbo igual, dos veces diez saetas.

No el polvo desparece
el campo, que no pisan alas hierba;
es el más torpe una herida cierva,
el más tardo la vista desvanece,
    y, siguiendo al más lento,
    cojea el pensamiento.

El tercio casi de una milla era
    la prolija carrera
que los hercúleos troncos hace breves;
1050   pero las plantas leves
    de tres sueltos zagales
la distancia sincopan tan iguales,
que la atención confunden judiciosa.

De la Peneida virgen desdeñosa,
los dulces fugitivos miembros bellos
en la corteza no abrazó, reciente,
más firme Apolo, más estrechamente,
que de una y otra meta gloriosa
las duras basas abrazaron ellos
1060   con triplicado nudo.
Árbitro Alcides en sus ramas, dudo
    que el caso decidiera,
bien que su menor hoja un ojo fuera
    del lince más agudo.

En tanto pues que el palio neutro pende
y la carroza de la luz desciende
a templarse en las ondas, Himeneo
– por templar, en los brazos, el deseo

Whose cords of steel or fibre are released
With one sharp hiss a score of arrows flies.　　　　1040

　　　They hide not as they pass
The fields in dust; wings do not tread on grass.
For like a wounded doe the heaviest flies,
The hindmost distances the watcher's eyes,
　　　The slowest leaves the mind
　　　Still limping far behind

Six hundred yards the long-drawn course extended,
　　　And far off where it ended
Tiny appeared those Herculean trees;
　　　But with light-footed ease　　　　1050
　　　Three mountain shepherds ran,
Abridging in such equal time the span
As baffled those who watched most warily.

Apollo clasped not with such urgency
Peneus' scornful maid, whom he embraced
Just as the flying limbs which he pursued
From fair soft flesh changed to unyielding wood,
As, when they reached their noble goal, the three
Clasped one or other stubborn trunk, in haste
　　　Their triple knot to tie.　　　　1060
Vainly from his own boughs the god would try
　　　To judge the case aright,
Even were his smallest leaf endowed with sight
　　　Sharp as a lynx's eye.

While, with the prize in doubt, the car of day
Descends to where the ocean's waves allay
Its fire, Hymen anticipates the haste
Of gallant groom and lovely bride, embraced

75

del galán novio, de la esposa bella –
1070 los rayos anticipa de la estrella,
cerúlea ahora, ya purpúrea guía
de los dudosos términos del día.

El júicio – al de todos, indeciso –
del concurso ligero,
el padrino con tres de limpio acero
cuchillos corvos absolvello quiso.
Solícita Junón, Amor no omiso,
al son de otra zampoña que conduce
ninfas bellas y sátiros lascivos,
1080 los desposados a su casa vuelven,
que coronada luce
de estrellas fijas, de astros fugitivos
que en sonoroso humo se resuelven.

Llegó todo el lugar, y, despedido,
casta Venus – que el lecho ha prevenido
de las plumas que baten más suaves
en su volante carro blancas aves –
los novios entra en dura no estacada:
que, siendo Amor una deidad alada,
1090 bien previno la hija de la espuma
a batallas de amor campo de pluma.

76

In straining arms, to allay the fire of love,
And sends the planet which presides above,   1070
Cerulean first, and then with purple light,
Over the dubious bounds of day and night.

No certain verdict on the hard-run race
        The wavering public gives,
But now the father, with three curving knives
Of shining steel, resolves the doubtful case.
Juno and Love, mindful of every grace,
While beauteous nymphs and lusty satyrs dance
Behind the music of another flute,
Bring back the wedded pair to their abode,   1080
        Crowned with the radiance
Of many stars, some fixed and some that shoot
Like meteors and in sounding smoke explode.

When all who followed on their way had sped,
And Venus had prepared the marriage bed
With plumage from the softest wings of white
Which beat the air before her car in flight,
The lovers to no hurtful lists she brings,
For, since her Cupid is a god with wings,
The daughter of the foam has wisely found   1090
Feathers are Love's most fitting battle-ground.

77

SOLEDAD SEGUNDA

Éntrase el mar por un arroyo breve
que a recibillo con sediento paso
de su roca natal se precipita,
y mucha sal no sólo en poco vaso,
    mas su ruina bebe,
y su fin, cristalina mariposa
    – no alada, sino undosa – ,
en el farol de Tetis solicita.

Muros desmantelando, pues, de arena,
centauro ya espumoso el océano
    – medio mar, medio ría –
dos veces huella la campaña al día,
escalar pretendiendo el monte en vano,
    de quien es dulce vena
    el tarde ya torrente
arrepentido, y aun retrocediente.

Eral lozano así novillo tierno,
    de bien nacido cuerno
    mal lunada la frente,
retrógrado cedió en desigual lucha
a duro toro, aun contra el viento armado:
    no pues de otra manera
    a la violencia mucha
del padre de las aguas, coronado
de blancas ovas y de espuma verde,
resiste obedeciendo, y tierra pierde.

SECOND SOLITUDE

A streamlet, rushing from its rocky shelf
In haste to slake its thirst where, surging up,
The tide invades its creek, drinks from the sea
Not only salt which fills its tiny cup,
    But ruin to itself,
And, like a crystal butterfly, with waves
    Instead of wings, it craves
From Thetis' lamp its final destiny.

Demolishing its walls of sand again,
Half river and half sea, the ocean's tide,   10
    A centaur of the spray,
Tramples across the land twice in a day,
And tries in vain to scale the mountainside
    Of which, a gentle vein,
    The torrent, sluggish now,
Repents, and even backward seems to flow.

A two-year bullock, bold but tender yet,
    Whose horns have scarcely set
    Their crescent on his brow,
Might well shrink backwards from the unequal course   20
With some fierce bull, armed to defy the wind.
    So did this stream, before
    The overwhelming force
Brought by the Father of all river-kind,
With green and white of wrack and spindrift crowned,
Resist while it obeyed, still losing ground.

En la incierta ribera
– guarnición desigual a tanto espejo – ,
descubrió la alba a nuestro peregrino
30   con todo el villanaje ultramarino,
que a la fiesta nupcial, de verde tejo
toldado, ya capaz tradujo pino.

Los escollos el sol rayaba, cuando,
    con remos gemidores,
dos pobres se aparecen pescadores,
nudos al mar de cáñamo fiando.
Ruiseñor en los bosques no más blando,
el verde robre que es barquillo ahora,
    saludar vió la Aurora,
40   que al uno en dulces quejas – y no pocas –
ondas endurecer, liquidar rocas.

Señas mudas la dulce voz doliente
    permitió solamente
a la turba, que dar quisiera voces
a la que de un ancón segunda haya
– cristal pisando azul con pies veloces –
salió improvisa, de una y otra playa
vínculo desatado, instable puente.

    La prora diligente
50   no sólo dirigió a la opuesta orilla,
mas redujo la música barquilla,
que en dos cuernos del mar caló no breves
sus plomos graves y sus corchos leves.

Los senos ocupó del mayor leño
    la marítima tropa,
    usando al entrar todos
cuantos les enseñó corteses modos

On this uncertain shore,
Unequal frame to mirror such a scene,
Dawn saw our pilgrim with a company
Of country folk, transported oversea   30
By a roomy pine-tree, canopied with green,
To grace the wedding-day's festivity.

Along the shore the cliffs in sunlight stood
      When two poor fishers who
Strained at their groaning oars came into view,
Their knotted hemp confiding to the flood.
Never at dawn did songbird in the wood
The living oak, now fashioned to a boat,
      Salute with sweeter note
Than one of these, whose many plaintive staves   40
Melted the rocks and petrified the waves.

With silent signs alone the sad sweet song
      Allowed the waiting throng
To hail a second vessel now in view
Which, from the inlet where it lay before,
Suddenly trod upon the crystal blue
With rapid feet, making from shore to shore
A floating bridge, a disconnected link.

      Towards the opposing brink
The industrious prow came on, and in its wake   50
It brought the tuneful bark, which seemed to slake
With the twin horns of sea through which it sped
Its many floats of cork and weights of lead.

The larger vessel for the seaborne troop
      Afforded ample space,
      And, as they entered, each
With all the courtesy of sailor speech

en la lengua del agua ruda escuela,
con nuestro forastero, que la popa
60   del canoro escogió bajel pequeño.

Aquél, las ondas escarchando, vuela;
éste, con perezoso movimiento,
el mar encuentra, cuya espuma cana
   su parda aguda prora
   resplandeciente cuello
hace de augusta Coya peruana,
a quien hilos el Sur tributó ciento
   de perlas cada hora.
Lágrimas no enjugó más de la aurora
70   sobre víolas negras la mañana,
que arrolló su espolón con pompa vana
caduco aljófar, pero aljófar bello.

Dando el huésped licencia para ello,
recurren no a las redes que, mayores,
mucho océano y pocas aguas prenden,
sino a las que ambiciosas menos penden,
   laberinto nudoso de marino
   Dédalo, si de leño no, de lino,
fábrica escrupulosa, y aunque incierta,
80   siempre murada, pero siempre abierta.

Liberalmente de los pescadores
al deseo el estero corresponde,
sin valelle al lascivo ostión el justo
   arnés de hueso, donde
   lisonja breve al gusto
   – mas incentiva – esconde:
contagio original quizá de aquella
   que, siempre hija bella

And simple schooling, spoke a greeting to
Our wanderer, who chose to take his place
Upon the smaller singing vessel's poop.   60

Whitening the surge with frost the former flew;
The other met the waves more lazily,
Which hung its pointed stem with beads of spray,
        And made the swarthy prow
        The shining neck of her
Who ruled the Incas, and for whose array
A hundred chains of pearls the southern sea
        Must every day bestow.
Never on dusky violets tears of dew
Were in such numbers dried at early day   70
As now the keel scattered in vain display
These transient pearls, yet pearls as white and fair.

Their guest's permission granted, they prepare
Their nets, but not the greater which comprise
Less depth of water than extent of sea,
But those which dangle less ambitiously,
Whose knotty labyrinth, with flax instead
Of wood, some ocean Daedalus first made,
Which, of precise yet dubious mesh composed,
Though always open yet is always closed.   80

Freely the estuary satisfies
The fishers' aspirations; uselessly
The lusty oyster strives, in mail encased
        Whose bony panoply
        Conceals a short-lived taste
        Of flattering piquancy.
Perhaps the daughter of the crystal wave
        The first infection gave,

83

de los cristales, una
90   venera fué su cuna.

Mallas visten de cáñamo al lenguado,
mientras, en su piel lúbrica fiado,
el congrio, que viscosamente liso,
    las telas burlar quiso,
tejido en ellas se quedó burlado.

Las redes califica menos gruesas,
    sin romper hilo alguno,
pompa el salmón de las reales mesas,
cuando no de los campos de Neptuno,
100   y el travieso robalo,
guloso de los cónsules regalo.

Estos y muchos más, unos desnudos,
otros de escamas fáciles armados,
    dió la ría pescados,
que, nadando en un piélago de nudos,
no agravan poco al negligente robre,
espaciosamente dirigido
al bienaventurado albergue pobre,
que, de carrizos frágiles tejido,
110   si fabricado no de gruesas cañas,
bóvedas lo coronan de espadañas.

El peregrino, pues, haciendo en tanto
instrumento el bajel, cuerdas los remos,
al céfiro encomienda los extremos
    deste métrico llanto:

    «Si de aire articulado
no son dolientes lágrimas suaves

Cradled among the swell
In a venereal shell.   90

The fluke with hempen meshes they invest,
While, trusting to his lissome body dressed
In slippery skin, the conger thinks the net
    Merely a jest, and yet,
Quickly involved, himself becomes the jest.

To grace the nets of finer mesh, whose cords
    Unbroken all remain,
The salmon enters, pomp of regal boards,
If not indeed of Neptune's watery plain,
    And wanton perch, long able   100
To furnish dainties for a gourmand's table.

All these and many more the firth allots
The fishers for their catch, some smooth of hide,
    Some lightly fortified
With scales, who, swimming in a sea of knots,
Disturb the ship which, to the lazy beat
Of casual rowers, moves with little speed
Towards a poor but fortunate retreat,
Whose walls are twisted out of fragile reed,
Sometimes with stouter rushes intertwined,   110
And with a dome of simple cat-tail crowned.

Meanwhile, his cares confiding to the breeze,
The boat his zither and the oars his strings,
The wanderer in plaintive numbers sings
    His grief's extremities.

    'If air articulate
Make not these sad sweet tears, then are the sighs

　　　　estas mis quejas graves,
voces de sangre, y sangre son del alma.
120　　　Fíelas de tu calma
¡oh mar! quien otra vez las ha fiado
de tu fortuna aun más que de su hado.

　　　　¡Oh mar, oh tú, supremo
moderador piadoso de mis daños!
　　　　tuyos serán mis años,
en tabla redimidos poco fuerte,
　　　　de la bebida muerte,
que ser quiso, en aquel peligro extremo,
ella el forzado y su guadaña el remo.

130　　　Regiones pise ajenas,
o clima propio, planta mía perdida,
　　　　tuya será mi vida,
si vida me ha dejado que sea tuya
　　　　quien me fuerza a que huya
de su prisión, dejando mis cadenas
rastro en tus ondas más que en tus arenas.

　　　　Audaz mi pensamiento
el cenit escaló, plumas vestido,
　　　　cuyo vuelo atrevido
140　　　– si no ha dado su nombre a tus espumas –
　　　　de sus vestidas plumas
conservarán el desvanecimiento
los anales diáfanos del viento.

　　　　Esta, pues, culpa mía
el timón alternar menos seguro
　　　　y el báculo más duro
un lustro ha hecho a mi dudosa mano,

That sound my miseries
Voices of blood, the inmost spirit's blood.
    To your now tranquil flood   120
He trusts them now, who trusted them of late
More to your chances than to his own fate.

    Ocean, who once before
Brought pitiful relief to all my tears,
    Yours are my future years,
For they were rescued from a brittle raft
    And Death's destructive draught,
Who made himself the slave, his scythe the oar,
That from dire peril brought me safe to shore.

    Whether a foreign strand   130
I tread, or reach again my native shores,
    My life shall still be yours,
If any life survive her cruelty
    Whose dungeons now I flee,
Leaving my chains to print their prison brand
Upon your waters rather than your sand.

    Once my presumptuous mind
Essayed, in feathers dressed, the zenith's height,
    But my foolhardy flight
Gave none of your domains a second name,   140
    And now the only fame
The scattered remnants of my plumage find
Is on the viewless annals of the wind.

    My doubtful hand still tries
Now the least trusty tiller, now the rough
    Wood of the hardest staff;
My guilt has sought in vain these five years past

solicitando en vano
las alas sepultar de mi osadía
150   donde el sol nace o donde muere el día.

Muera, enemiga amada,
muera mi culpa, y tu desdén le guarde,
    arrepentido tarde,
suspiro que mi muerte haga leda,
    cuando no le suceda,
o por breve o por tibia o por cansada,
lágrima antes enjuta que llorada.

Naufragio ya segundo,
o filos pongan de homicida hierro
160   fin duro a mi destierro;
tan generosa fe, no fácil onda,
    no poca tierra esconda:
urna suya el Océano profundo,
y obeliscos los montes sean del mundo.

Túmulo tanto debe
agradecido Amor a mi pie errante;
    líquido, pues, diamante
calle mis huesos, y elevada cima
    selle sí, mas no oprima,
170   esta que le fiaré ceniza breve,
si hay ondas mudas y si hay tierra leve.»

No es sordo el mar: la erudición engaña.
    Bien que tal vez sañudo
no oya al piloto, o le responda fiero,
sereno disimula más orejas
    que sembró dulces quejas
– canoro labrador – el forastero
    en su undosa campaña.

Some pit wherein to cast
The wings of my audacious enterprise,
Either where day is born or sunset dies.   150

O let my fault be dead,
Dear enemy; if from your contrite scorn
    A tardy sigh is born
My death will be the sweeter, even though
    You care not to bestow
(Chary, reluctant and uninterested)
A tear that's dry almost before it's shed.

Whether a second squall
Drown me, or some assassin's keen-edged knife
    Abridge my banished life,   160
No common earth my generous faith can hold,
    No trivial wave enfold:
All Ocean's depths must be its urn, and all
Earth's mountains stand for its memorial.

Let grateful Love requite
My wandering steps with such a tomb, and grant
    That liquid adamant
Silence my bones, sealed by some soaring crest,
    Yet not too rudely pressed
On dust, confided to your depth and height,   170
If ocean can be dumb or earth be light.'

The ocean is not deaf; the sage deceives.
    Enraged, it seldom hears
The pilot, else a fierce reply bestows,
Yet hides, when calm, more ears beneath its surges
    Than all the gentle dirges
Which, tuneful husbandman, the wanderer sows
    Upon its field of waves.

89

Espongioso, pues, se bebió y mudo
180 el lagrimoso reconocimiento,
de cuyos dulces números no poca
        concentuosa suma
en los dos giros de invisible pluma
que fingen sus dos alas, hurtó el viento;
Eco – vestida una cavada roca –
solicitó curiosa y guardó avara
la más dulce – si no la menos clara –
        sílaba, siendo en tanto
la vista de las chozas fin del canto.

190 Yace en el mar, si no continuada,
isla mal de la tierra dividida,
cuya forma tortuga es perezosa:
díganlo cuantos siglos ha que nada
sin besar de la playa espaciosa
la arena, de las ondas repetida.

A pesar, pues, del agua que la oculta,
concha, si mucha no, capaz ostenta
de albergues, donde la humildad contenta
mora, y Pomona se venera culta.

200 Dos son las chozas, pobre su artificio
más aún que caduca su materia:
de los mancebos dos, la mayor, cuna;
de las redes la otra y su ejercicio,
        competente oficina.
Lo que agradable más se determina
del breve islote, ocupa su fortuna,
los extremos de fausto y de miseria
moderando.

The sea, silent and spongy, drank the tears
Of these acknowledgments; and much likewise　　　　180
Of the harmonious sum these numbers made
　　　With twofold flutterings
Was stolen by the two imagined wings
On which the wind with unseen feathers flies;
While Echo, in a rocky cave arrayed,
Eagerly sought and greedily possessed
The sweetest words, if not the tenderest,
　　　Until a nearer view
Discerned the huts and stopped the singing too.

An island, not continuing the land,　　　　190
Yet barely separate, lies in the sea,
Shaped like a tortoise, and a lazy one,
For it has not yet kissed the spacious sand
Across the strait, though tides have come and gone
While it has swum there many a century.

But little of the hidden shell appeared
Above the waves, and yet that little showed
Cabins in which Humility abode
Contented, and Pomona was revered.

Two huts there are, even lowlier in design　　　　200
Than frail of structure; for the youthful pair
Cradle and home the larger cot supplies;
The smaller for the care of line and net
　　　An ample space provides;
And what the tiny isle affords besides
Of fertile land, their fortune occupies,
Tempering the extremes of needy care
And sumptuous wealth.

En la plancha los recibe
el padre de los dos, émulo cano
210   del sagrado Nereo, no ya tanto
porque a la par de los escollos vive,
porque en el mar preside comarcano
al ejercicio piscatorio, cuanto
por seis hijas, por seis deidades bellas,
del cielo espumas y del mar estrellas.

Acogió al huésped con urbano estilo,
y a su voz, que los juncos obedecen,
tres hijas suyas cándidas le ofrecen,
que engaños construyendo están de hilo.
220   El huerto le da esotras, a quien debe
si púrpura la rosa, el lilio nieve.

De jardín culto así en fingida gruta,
salteó al labrador pluvia improvisa
de cristales inciertos, a la seña,
o a la que torció llave el fontanero:
urna de Acuario, la imitada peña
lo embiste incauto; y si con pie grosero
para la fuga apela, nubes pisa,
burlándolo aun la parte más enjuta.

230   La vista saltearon poco menos
del huésped admirado
las no líquidas perlas, que, al momento,
a los corteses juncos – porque el viento
nudos les halle un día, bien que ajenos –
el cáñamo remiten anudado,
y de Vertumno al término labrado
el breve hierro, cuyo corvo diente
las plantas le mordía cultamente.

To welcome them on land
The father came, a greybeard who might vie
With god-like Nereus, not so much because   210
He lived among the rocks that fence the strand
And governed all the neighbouring clans who ply
The fisher's trade, but that the sire he was
Of six fair daughters, six divinities
Like sky-tossed foam or starlight on the seas.

A courteous greeting to the guest he proffered;
The reeds obeyed his voice and, opening,
Revealed three shining maids, who wove with string
Deceitful meshes; then the garden offered
The other three, to whom the rose might owe   220
Its crimson and the daffodil its snow.

Grottos contrived in curious gardens may
Entrap the peasant in unlooked-for floods
Of dubious crystals when, apprised by some
Signal, the fountain-keeper turns his key,
And seeming rocks, assailing him, become
Aquarius' urn, and if he turns to flee
His awkward footsteps seem to tread on clouds,
Deceived by what he thought the driest way.

The guest, surprised too, wondered at the view   230
Of these fair pearls, though not
Liquid, and who, in order that the wind
For once might knots among the rushes find,
Though alien ones, had now confided to
The courteous reeds the knotted hemp they wrought,
Or to Vertumnus' cultivated plot
Resigned the pruning-hook whose curving tooth,
Biting the plants, encourages their growth.

Ponderador saluda afectuoso
240   del esplendor que admira el extranjero
al sol, en seis luceros dividido;
y – honestamente al fin correspondido
    del coro vergonzoso –
al viejo sigue, que prudente ordena
los términos confunda de la cena
la comida prolija de pescados,
raros muchos, y todos no comprados.

Impidiéndole el día al forastero,
con dilaciones sordas le divierte
250   entre unos verdes carrizales, donde
armonioso número se esconde
de blancos cisnes, de la misma suerte
que gallinas domésticas al grano,
a la voz concurrientes del anciano.

En la más seca, en la más limpia anea
vivificando están muchos sus huevos,
y mientras dulce aquél su muerte anuncia
    entre la verde juncia,
sus pollos éste al mar conduce nuevos,
260   de Espío y de Nerea
– cuando más obscurecen las espumas –
nevada invidia, sus nevadas plumas.

Hermana de Faetón, verde el cabello,
les ofrece el que, joven ya gallardo,
de flexuosas mimbres garbín pardo
tosco le ha encordonado, pero bello.
Lo más liso trepó, lo más sublime
venció su agilidad, y artificiosa
tejió en sus ramas inconstantes nidos

The observant stranger failed not to admire
The splendour of this sun with six-fold ray;   240
Giving them kindly greeting, which at once
Was equalled by the no less frank response
    Made by the modest choir,
He followed the old man, whose wisdom changed
The normal hour of supper, and arranged
A long-drawn-out repast with numerous dishes
Of many rare, but all unpurchased, fishes.

The father then, to while away the day,
With pleasant converse kept his guest amused
Where, in green rushes by the water's side   250
Swans in harmonious numbers strove to hide
Their plumes of white, yet seemed as much disposed
To assemble when they heard the old man's tone
As barnyard fowls to whom their grain is thrown.

Quickening their eggs, many there are who dwell
Among the cleanest and the driest sedge;
One from the verdant reeds with sad sweet lay
    Proclaims his latest day;
One leads her cygnets to the ocean's edge:
    The Nereids might well,   260
Even when they most outshine the foaming seas,
Covet the snow of snowy plumes like these.

Phaëthon's green-haired daughter showed them what
In sprightly youth the sire had plaited her,
A dark grey coif of sinewy osier
Which, rudely twisted, yet was fairly wrought.
He climbed the smoothest trunk, the tallest tree
Nimbly he conquered, and he wove between
The boughs with cunning hand the changeful nests

95

270   donde celosa arrulla y ronca gime
      la ave lasciva de la cipria diosa.
      Mástiles coronó menos crecidos,
      gavia no tan capaz: extraño todo,
      el designio, la fábrica y el modo.

      A pocos pasos le admiró no menos
      montecillo, las sienes laureado,
      traviesos despidiendo moradores
          de sus confusos senos,
      conejuelos, que – el viento consultado –
280   salieron retozando a pisar flores:
      el más tímido, al fin, más ignorante
          del plomo fulminante.

      Cóncavo fresno – a quien gracioso indulto
      de su caduco natural permite
      que a la encina vivaz robusto imite,
      y hueco exceda al alcornoque inculto –
      verde era pompa de un vallete oculto,
      cuando frondoso alcázar no, de aquella,
      que sin corona vuela y sin espada,
290   susurrante amazona, Dido alada,
      de ejército más casto, de más bella
      república, ceñida, en vez de muros,
      de cortezas; en esta, pues, Cartago
      reina la abeja, oro brillando vago,
      o el jugo beba de los aires puros,
      o el sudor de los cielos, cuando liba
      de las mudas estrellas la saliva;
      burgo eran suyo el tronco informe, el breve
      corcho, y moradas pobres sus vacíos,
300   del que más solicita los desvíos
      de la isla, plebeyo enjambre leve.

Where, moaning harshly, cooing jealously,   270
Lodges the amorous bird of Cypria's queen.
Tall vessels often crown less lofty masts
With smaller topsails; all was strange and new,
Design and handiwork and fashion too.

No less a little mountain close at hand
The youth admires, its brows with laurel twined,
Which from the mazes of its bosom pours
     A lively native band,
Rabbits who, snuffing counsel from the wind,
Gambol and scurry over grass and flowers;   280
Even the most timid feels least need to dread
     The thunderbolt of lead.

Spared by a gracious truce the natural fate
Of failing age, a concave ash outvied
The giant cork in hollow growth, and tried
The oak tree's vigorous strength to emulate.
A hidden vale it clothed in verdant state,
And made a leafy castle too for her
Who, though she flies with neither sword nor crown,
A wing-borne Dido, rustling Amazon,   290
Leads chaster armies, rules a lovelier
Kingdom, with cork-bark girt instead of walls,
A veritable Carthage where the bee
Is queen, shining with wandering gold as she
From the pure ether drinks the juice that falls,
Or sucks the effluence of the sky, or sips
Saliva from the silent stars that drips.
They have their city in this rugged tree,
And in its slender hollow bark they form
Their humble homes, this swift plebeian swarm   300
That seek the isle's remote extremity.

Llegaron luego donde al mar se atreve,
si promontorio no, un cerro elevado,
  de cabras estrellado,
  iguales, aunque pocas,
a la que – imagen décima del cielo –
flores su cuerno es, rayos su pelo.

«Éstas», dijo el isleño venerable,
«y aquéllas que, pendientes de las rocas,
310 tres o cuatro desean para ciento,
– redil las ondas y pastor el viento –
libres discurren, su nocivo diente
paz hecha con las plantas inviolable.»

Estimando seguía el peregrino
  al venerable isleño,
de muchos pocos numeroso dueño,
cuando los suyos enfrenó de un pino
el pie villano, que groseramente
los cristales pisaba de una fuente.

320 Ella, pues, sierpe, y sierpe al fin pisada,
– aljófar vomitando fugitivo
  en lugar de veneno –
torcida esconde, ya que no enroscada,
las flores, que de un parto dió lascivo
aura fecunda al matizado seno
del huerto, en cuyos troncos se desata
de las escamas que vistió de plata.

Seis chopos, de seis yedras abrazados,
tirsos eran del griego dios, nacido
330 segunda vez, que en pámpanos desmiente
  los cuernos de su frente;

They reach a place where there affronts the sea
A lofty bluff, if not a headland, starred
   With goats, a scanty herd,
   Yet rivalling the bright
Tenth image of the sky, whose hide and horn
Such brilliant rays and plenteous flowers adorn.

'These,' said the worthy islander, 'and those
That hang above us on the rocky height
Make up a hundred, all save two or three;   310
The wind their shepherd and their fold the sea,
They run at large, their hurtful tooth perforce
At peace with vines, for here no vine-shoot grows.'

The youth beside the reverend islesman walked,
   Esteeming him as lord
Of a both numerous and trivial hoard,
When by an oak-tree's foot his own was blocked,
Which clumsily bestrode a streamlet's course
And rudely trampled on the crystal source.

Snake-like, and like a trodden snake it glides,   320
But transient pearls of spray it vomits forth
   Instead of venomed rheum;
With many a twist and turn the flowers it hides,
Which fertile breezes in a tender birth
Breed from the garden's many-coloured womb,
And loosens to the tree-trunks of the glade
The silver scales in which it is arrayed.

Six poplar trees, embraced by ivy, stand
Like thyrsi of the twice-born Grecian god,
Who twines his brow with vine-leaves, that the wreath 330
   May hide the horns beneath.

99

y cual mancebos tejen anudados
festivos corros en alegre ejido,
coronan ellos el encanecido
suelo de lilios, que en fragantes copos
nevó el mayo, a pesar de los seis chopos.

Este sitio las bellas seis hermanas
    escogen, agraviando
en breve espacio mucha primavera
340 con las mesas, cortezas ya livianas
del árbol que ofreció a la edad primera
duro alimento, pero sueño blando.

Nieve hilada, y por sus manos bellas
caseramente a telas reducida,
    manteles blancos fueron.
Sentados, pues, sin ceremonias, ellas
en torneado fresno la comida
    con silencio sirvieron.

Rompida el agua en las menudas piedras,
350 cristalina sonante era tiorba,
y las confusamente acordes aves,
entre las verdes roscas de las yedras,
muchas eran, y muchas veces nueve
aladas musas, que – de pluma leve
engañada su oculta lira corva –
metros inciertos sí, pero suaves,
en idiomas cantan diferentes;
mientras, cenando en pórfidos lucientes,
    lisonjean apenas
360 al Júpiter marino tres sirenas.

Comieron, pues, y rudamente dadas
gracias el pescador a la divina

As on some merry heath a youthful band
Weave mazy circles in their festive mood,
So the six trees with branches crown the sod
Frosted with lilies, snowed by May, despite
The poplars' shade, in flakes of fragrant white.

Here, in the little space which presently
        The six fair sisters chose,
Great was the wealth of spring their tables grieved,
Fashioned of finest cork-bark, from that tree   340
Whence in the primal age our sires received
Harsh nourishment, but sound and sweet repose.

Snow, which the sisters' own fair hands had spun,
By homely craft woven to linen sheets,
        They spread for napery,
Then, seated unaffectedly, upon
Platters of well-turned ash they placed the meats
        And served them silently.

The water, eddying round the tiny stones,
Played on a crystalline theorbo's strings;   350
Among the ivy's verdant coils there rang
The birds' confused and yet harmonious tones;
Many they were, and many times their choirs
Surpassed the nine winged Muses – curving lyres
Disguised beneath their lightly feathered wings –
And sweetly, if uncertainly, they sang
Each in his diverse tongue; while in the sea,
Supping on thrones of lucent porphyry,
        Three sirens vainly strove
To please the ear of ocean-ruling Jove.   360

The meal was over, and the father said
A simple prayer of thanks to the divine

próvida mano, «¡Oh bien vividos años!
¡Oh canas», dijo el huésped, «no peinadas
con boj dentado o con rayada espina,
sino con verdaderos desengaños!
Pisad dichoso esta esmeralda bruta,
en mármol engastada siempre undoso,
jubilando la red en los que os restan
370   felices años, y la humedecida
        o poco rato enjuta
próxima arena de esa opuesta playa,
        la remota Cambaya
sea de hoy más a vuestro leño ocioso;
y el mar que os la divide, cuanto cuestan
        Océano importuno
a las Quinas – del viento aun veneradas –
        sus ardientes veneros,
su esfera lapidosa de luceros.

380   Del pobre albergue a la barquilla pobre,
geómetra prudente, el orbe mida
        vuestra planta, impedida
– si de purpúreas conchas, no, istriadas –
de trágicas ruinas de alto robre,
que – el tridente acusando de Neptuno –
        menos quizá dió astillas
que ejemplos de dolor a estas orillas.»

«Días ha muchos, oh mancebo», dijo
        el pescador anciano,
390   «que en el uno cedí y el otro hermano
el duro remo, el cáñamo prolijo;
        muchos ha dulces días
que cisnes me recuerdan a la hora
        que huyendo la Aurora

Providing hand, and then: 'O well-lived years!'
The youth exclaimed. 'O venerable head,
Which not with dented box or thorny spine
But disenchantment combs its greying hair!
Walk, well content, this uncut emerald set
In undulating marble, and allow
The net to rest through whatsoever Fate
Still grants of happy years. The neighbouring sand   370
      Which, scarcely dried, is wet
On the opposing shore, be far away
      As is remote Cathay
From this time onward to your idle prow.
This narrow sound seem the importunate
      Flood which the Portuguese,
Whom even the wind reveres, have crossed to tear
      Ore from the burning mine,
Stars from the sphere where stony clusters shine.

Pacing from this frail hut to that frail bark,   380
Prudent geometer, measure the land,
      Less hindered where the strand
Is strewn with fluted purple shells than where
Once lofty oaks, in tragic ruin stark,
Accuse his trident who commands the seas,
      And fewer splinters strow
Upon these shores than auguries of woe.'

'Many a day,' the ancient fisher said,
      'O youth, has now gone by
Since to the one and other brother I   390
Resigned the prolix hemp, the weary blade.
      Many sweet days the swan
Has waked me, and Aurora, having fled
      Tithonus' whitened head,

las canas de Titón, halla las mías,
a pesar de mi edad, no en la alta cumbre
de aquel morro difícil, cuyas rocas
tarde o nunca pisaron cabras pocas,
y milano venció con pesadumbre,
400   sino desotro escollo al mar pendiente;
de donde ese teatro de Fortuna
descubro, ese voraz, ese profundo
campo ya de sepulcros, que, sediento,
cuanto, en vasos de abeto, Nuevo Mundo
– tributos digo américos – se bebe
en túmulos de espuma paga breve.

Bárbaro observador, mas diligente,
de las inciertas formas de la Luna,
a cada conjunción su pesquería,
410   y a cada pesquería su instrumento
– más o menos nudoso – atribuído,
mis hijos dos en un batel despido,
que, el mar cribando en redes no comunes,
vieras intempestivos algún día
– entre un vulgo nadante, digno apenas
de escama, cuanto más de nombre – atunes
vomitar ondas y azotar arenas.

Tal vez desde los muros destas rocas
        cazar a Tetis veo
420   y pescar a Diana en dos barquillas:
náuticas venatorias maravillas
de mis hijas oirás, ambiguo coro,
menos de aljaba que de red armado,
        de cuyo, si no alado,
harpón vibrante, supo mal Proteo
en globos de agua redimir sus focas.

Upon my hoary locks in turn has shone,
Walking, despite my age, not on that height
So steep that on its rocky top the goat
Seldom or never sets its nimble foot,
And hard of conquest even by the kite,
But on that other, jutting from the strand,   400
Whence I survey this Fortune's theatre,
This ravenous, profound and thirsty field
Of sepulchres, which drains from cups of pine
Whatever spoils America may yield –
The New World's gifts – and grants no more in pay
Than momentary catafalques of spray.

Diligent, if untutored, I have scanned
The uncertain motions of the lunar sphere;
To every phase I know what fish belong,
And can to every fish the gear assign,   410
Ordering more or fewer knots, that so
My sons with far from common nets may go
To sift the ocean from their tiny boat;
And you may see some day, swimming among
The lesser breeds, unworthy name or scales,
Great tunny-fish, unseasonably caught,
Who belch out watery floods and lash their tails.

Diana fishing, Thetis at the chase
    I sometimes have descried
From these high walls of rock, each in her boat.   420
My daughters' venatorial feats afloat
Hear and admire – ambiguous company,
Who sling no quivers more than net they bear,
    Yet from their vibrant spear,
Though wingless, Proteus vainly tries to hide
Among his watery globes the phocine race.

Torpe la más veloz, marino toro,
torpe, mas toro al fin, que el mar violado
de la púrpura viendo de sus venas,
430   bufando mide el campo de las ondas
con la animosa cuerda, que prolija
al hierro sigue que en la foca huye,
o grutas ya la privilegien hondas,
o escollos desta isla divididos:
Láquesis nueva mi gallarda hija,
si Cloto no de la escamada fiera,
ya hila, ya devana su carrera,
cuando desatinada pide, o cuando
        vencida restituye
440   los términos de cáñamo pedidos.

Rindióse al fin la bestia, y las almenas
de las sublimes rocas salpicando,
las peñas embistió peña escamada,
en ríos de agua y sangre desatada.

Éfire luego – la que en el torcido
luciente nácar te sirvió no poca
risueña parte de la dulce fuente –
de Filódoces émula valiente,
cuya asta breve desangró la foca,
450   el cabello en estambre azul cogido
– celoso alcaide de sus trenzas de oro –
en segundo bajel se engolfó sola.

¡Cuántas voces le di! ¡Cuántas en vano
tiernas derramé lágrimas, temiendo,
no al fiero tiburón, verdugo horrendo
del náufrago ambicioso mercadante,

Sluggish the swiftest ocean bull might be,
Sluggish, but still a bull, when far and near
It saw the ocean purpled from its veins
And, snorting, measured out the field of waves   430
With the prolix and lively cord it drew
Reaved to the very dart from which it fled,
Whether it sheltered deep in ocean caves,
Or in the shoals most from the isle remote.
A Lachesis, if not a Clotho new,
My gallant child was to the savage seal,
Now paying out, now winding back the reel,
As first in rage it sought the full extent,
        And then, discomfited,
Restored the hempen limits it had sought.   440

Surrendering at last, the monster stains
The soaring cliff's sublimest battlement;
Rock-like it now assails the rocky shore,
Dissolved in watery floods and streams of gore.

Then Éfire, who lately proffered you
In shining cup of twisted nacreous shell
The smiling fountain's sweet and copious draught,
Emulous of Filódoces, whose shaft
Had made the wound from which the monster fell,
Her head encircled with a band of blue   450
That kept her golden tresses jealously,
Dared in a second boat alone to sail.

How many tender tears in vain I shed!
How many shouts I uttered! Not in fear
Of some fierce shark, grim executioner
Of merchants by their fond ambitions wrecked,

ni al otro cuyo nombre
espada es tantas veces esgrimida
contra mis redes ya, contra mi vida:
460   sino algún siempre verde, siempre cano
sátiro de las aguas, petulante
violador del virginal decoro,
marino dios, que – el vulto feroz, hombre –
corvo es delfín la cola.

Sorda a mis voces, pues, ciega a mi llanto,
abrazado, si bien de fácil cuerda,
un plomo fió grave a un corcho leve;
que algunas veces despedido cuanto
– penda o nade – la vista no lo pierda,
470   el golpe solicita, el bulto mueve
prodigiosos moradores ciento
del líquido elemento.

Láminas uno de viscoso acero
– rebelde aun al diamante – el duro lomo
hasta el luciente bipartido extremo
de la cola vestido,
solicitado sale del ruido;
y al cebarse en el cómplice ligero
del suspendido plomo,
480   Éfire, en cuya mano al flaco remo
un fuerte dardo había sucedido,
de la mano a las ondas gemir hizo
el aire con el fresno arrojadizo;
de las ondas al pez, con vuelo mudo,
deidad dirigió amante el hierro agudo:
entre una y otra lámina, salida
la sangre halló por do la muerte entrada.

Nor him whose name implies
The sword, so often aimed in deadly strife
To cut my nets and to destroy my life;
Some ocean satyr, ever hoar of head   460
And ever green of form, did I expect,
Vile ravisher of maiden chastity,
Sea-god whose savage human face belies
    A dolphin's curving tail.

Deaf to my cries, alas, blind to my woe,
Held by a slender cord, she trusted to
A flimsy cork with heavy plummet armed
Which, many times plunged in the waves below
To float or swim, but ever kept in view,
Lured with its splash or with its bulk alarmed   470
The hundred monstrous dwellers who frequent
    The liquid element.

One who in viscid plates of steel, too hard
For diamond to cut, was habited
From stalwart back to where the cloven tip
    Flashed in the outmost rear,
Now by the noise incited to appear,
Snatched at the light accomplice of the cord
    That held the pendant lead.
Then Éfire relinquished from her grip   480
The feeble oar, and grasped a sturdy spear,
Causing the air, through which the ash was thrown
Between her fingers and the waves, to moan,
On which, from wave to fish, in silent flight
Some favouring god guided the shaft aright;
Between two scales the pointed steel struck home,
And blood gushed out where death had made a door.

Onda, pues, sobre onda levantada,
montes de espuma concitó herida
490   la fiera, horror del agua, cometiendo
ya a la violencia, ya a la fuga el modo
    de sacudir el asta,
que, alterando el abismo o discurriendo
    el Océano todo,
no perdona al acero que la engasta.

Éfire en tanto al cáñamo torcido
el cabo rompió, y – bien que al ciervo herido
el can sobra, siguiéndole la flecha –
volvíase, mas no muy satisfecha,
500   cuando cerca de aquel peinado escollo
hervir las olas vió templadamente,
bien que haciendo círculos perfetos;
escogió, pues, de cuatro o cinco abetos
el de cuchilla más resplandeciente,
que atravesado remolcó un gran sollo.

    Desembarcó triunfando,
y aun el siguiente sol no vimos, cuando
en la ribera vimos convecina
dado al través el monstro, donde apenas
510   su género noticia, pías arenas
en tanta playa halló tanta ruina.»

    Aura en esto marina
el discurso, y el día juntamente,
trémula, si veloz, les arrebata,
alas batiendo líquidas, y en ellas
    dulcísimas querellas
de pescadores dos, de dos amantes
en redes ambos y en edad iguales.

Piling with wave on wave the watery floor,
And raising mountain peaks of boiling foam,
The wounded terror of the waters tried   490
To extricate the spear by force or flight,
    But yet, no matter how
It thrashed the depths or scoured the ocean wide,
    The shaft would not respite
The plates of steel that formed its setting now.

The twisted hempen cord that held the spear
Éfire cut, and since the wounded deer
Needs not the hound after the shaft has struck,
She turned, though ill contented with her luck,
Then as she passed the gentle ebb and flow   500
Around that polished head of rock, and saw
The perfect circles that its motion made,
From four or five harpoons she chose the blade
That shone most brightly, which she hurled, to draw
A massive sturgeon back, transfixed, in tow.

    Triumphantly she landed,
And on the neighbouring shore we saw the stranded
Monster before we saw the morning rays:
So strange that we could scarcely guess its kind,
So huge its ruined bulk could hardly find   510
A resting place on sands so wide as these.'

    And now an ocean breeze,
Tremulous but rapid, ended their discourse,
And likewise brought the ending of the day,
Bearing upon the liquid wings it beat
    Complaints which, soft and sweet,
Two fishers made, two lovers, equal both
In years and usage of the net as well.

Dividiendo cristales,
520   en la mitad de un óvalo de plata,
venía a tiempo el nieto de la espuma
que los mancebos daban alternantes
al viento quejas. Órganos de pluma
   – aves digo de Leda –
tales no oyó el Caístro en su arboleda,
tales no vió el Meandro en su corriente.
Inficionando pues suavemente
las ondas el Amor, sus flechas remos,
hasta donde se besan los extremos
530   de la isla y del agua no los deja.

Lícidas, gloria en tanto
de la playa, Micón de sus arenas
   – invidia de sirenas,
   convocación su canto
de músicos delfines, aunque mudos –
   en números no rudos
   el primero se queja
   de la culta Leucipe,
décimo esplendor bello de Aganipe;
540   de Cloris el segundo,
escollo de cristal, meta del mundo.

LÍCIDAS

¿A qué piensas, barquilla,
pobre ya cuna de mi edad primera,
que cisne te conduzgo a esta ribera?
A cantar dulce, y a morirme luego.
   Si te perdona el fuego
que mis huesos vinculan, en su orilla,
tumba te bese el mar, vuelta la quilla.

Parting the crystal swell
There now approached the grandson of the spray,   520
Who from his silver semi-oval heard
The sad alternate song which either youth
Gave to the wind. Akin to Leda's bird,
      Plumed organs such as these
Were never heard to sing on Caister's trees,
Or seen to float along Meander's course.
Cupid meanwhile, his arrows turned to oars,
Spreading their sweet contagion on the seas,
Followed, as far as the extremities
Where isle and ocean kiss, the tuneful pair.   530

      Lycidas, of the shore,
As of the sands Micón, the joy and pride
      – The envious sirens sighed
      To hear their singing lure
The dolphins, ever musical though mute –
      One pressed his tender suit
      In plaintive tones on fair
      Leucippe, who might bring
A tenth fair lustre to the Muses' spring,
      And one for Chloris pined,   540
A crystal rock, the goal of all mankind.

LYCIDAS

      Say, little boat that gave
My earliest years a cradle rough and poor,
Why, swanlike, have I steered you to this shore?
Sweetly to sing, perhaps, and then to die.
      If haply pardoned by
The fire my bones imprison, then the wave
Shall kiss your upturned keel that makes my grave.

113

MICÓN

Cansado leño mío,
550   hijo del bosque y padre de mi vida
– de tus remos ahora conducida
a desatarse en lágrimas cantando –,
    el doliente, si blando,
curso del llanto métrico te fío,
nadante urna de canoro río.

LÍCIDAS

    Las rugosas veneras
– fecundas no de aljófar blanco el seno,
ni del que enciende el mar tirio veneno –
entre crespos buscaba caracoles,
560   cuando de tus dos soles
fulminado, ya señas no ligeras
de mis cenizas dieron tus riberas.

MICÓN

    Distinguir sabía apenas
el menor leño de la mayor urca
que velera un Neptuno y otro surca,
y tus prisiones ya arrastraba graves;
    si dudas lo que sabes,
lee cuanto han impreso en tus arenas,
a pesar de los vientos, mis cadenas.

LÍCIDAS

570   Las que el cielo mercedes
hizo a mi forma, ¡oh dulce mi enemiga!
lisonja no, serenidad lo diga
de limpia consultada ya laguna,
    y los de mi fortuna

MICÓN

O weary timber, sprung
From forest sires, father of life and bread,   550
Upon this shore, whither your oars have led,
In my own tears dissolving as I sing,
    To you this sad sweet spring
Of plaintive melody must now belong,
O floating urn, in which I pour my song.

LYCIDAS

    I heaped a childish store,
Among the twisted snails, of fluted shells
(Not those whose breast with pearly whiteness swells,
Nor those whose poison dyes the seas of Tyre),
    Till, thunderstruck with fire   560
From your twin suns, I scattered even more
Ashes to be my relics on your shore.

MICÓN

    Too young to understand
Whether I saw some tiny skiff, or some
Vast whale that swiftly furrowed either foam,
Your heavy chains already clogged my going;
    But if you doubt, while knowing,
Read how my fetters have impressed their brand
Too deep for winds to raze them from your sand.

LYCIDAS

    Such grace as heaven decrees   570
My form, sweet foe, is no vain flattery;
The limpid mere, consulted, answers me
From its smooth surface, and the waves can tell
    My worldly gains as well,

privilegios, el mar a quien di redes,
más que a la selva lazos Ganimedes.

MICÓN

No ondas, no luciente
cristal – agua al fin dulcemente dura – :
invidia califique mi figura
580   de musculosos jóvenes desnudos.
Menos dió al bosque nudos
que yo al mar, el que a un dios hizo valiente
mentir cerdas, celoso espumar diente.

LÍCIDAS

Cuantos pedernal duro
bruñe nácares boto, agudo raya
en la oficina undosa desta playa,
tantos Palemo a su Licore bella
suspende, y tantos ella
al flaco da, que me construyen muro,
590   junco frágil, carrizo mal seguro.

MICÓN

Las siempre desiguales
blancas primero ramas, después rojas,
del árbol que, nadante, ignoró hojas,
trompa Tritón del agua, a la alta gruta
de Nísida tributa,
ninfa por quien lucientes son corales
los rudos troncos hoy de mis umbrales.

LÍCIDAS

Esta, en plantas no escrita,
en piedras sí, firmeza honre Himeneo,

For I have cast more nets among the seas
Than Ganymede his nooses on the trees.

MICÓN

    By no clear pool apprised
Nor crystal (which is water sweetly hard),
My mirror is the envious regard
Of youthful athletes, muscular and nude.   580
    Fewer knots he gave the wood
Than I the sea, whom jealous Mars chastised
With bristling hide and foaming tusks disguised.

LYCIDAS

    What nacreous gems he found,
Which on this beach, the workshop of the wave,
The blunt flints burnish and the sharp engrave,
Palemus on Lycoris' charms bestowed,
    But with the precious load
The walls of my poor hut, but feebly bound
With fragile reed and yielding rush, she crowned.   590

MICÓN

    The ever varying boughs,
First white, then turned to crimson, of the tree
Which, swimming, knows not any greenery,
Triton, the trumpet of the ocean, gave
    Nisida's lofty cave,
The nymph through whom that shining coral glows
On the rough-timbered lintel of my house.

LYCIDAS

    My faith, carved deep and sure
On stone, not bark, may Hymen now approve,

600 calzándole talares mi deseo:
que el tiempo vuela. Goza, pues, ahora
    los lilios de tu aurora,
que al tramontar del sol mal solicita
abeja, aun negligente, flor marchita.

MICÓN

    Si fe tanta no en vano
desafía las rocas donde, impresa,
con labio alterno mucho mar la besa,
nupcial la califique tea luciente.
    Mira que la edad miente,
610 mira que del almendro más lozano
Parca es interior breve gusano.

Invidia convocaba, si no celo,
    al balcón de zafiro
las claras, aunque etíopes, estrellas,
    y las Osas dos bellas,
    sediento siempre tiro
del carro perezoso, honor del cielo;
    mas ¡ay! que del ruido
    de la sonante esfera,
620 a la una luciente y otra fiera
el piscatorio cántico impedido,
con las prendas bajaran de Cefeo
    a las vedadas ondas,
si Tetis no, desde sus grutas hondas,
    enfrenara el deseo.

¡Oh, cuánta al peregrino el amebeo
alterno canto dulce fué lisonja!
¿Qué mucho, si avarienta ha sido esponja

Winging his sandals to requite my love.   600
The moments fly; enjoy while there is time
      The lilies of your prime:
However careless, when the sunset hour
Is past, no bee will sip the withered flower.

      MICÓN

      If not in vain my faith
Defies the rocks on which it stands impressed,
By ocean's alternating lip caressed,
May nuptial torches shed a timely glow;
      For age deceives, and though
Profuse the almond bloom, the worm beneath   610
Gnaws, like a hidden Fate, the way to death.

Now to the sapphire balcony again
      Envy or jealousy
Summoned the bright, though Ethiopian stars
      And the two lovely Bears
      Who, thirsting endlessly,
Pride of the heavens, draw the sluggish Wain.
      But for the noise that rang
      From the resounding sphere
Nor one nor other shining beast could hear   620
The piscatorial strain their rivals sang.
To plunge, with Cepheus' pledges, they had sought
      In the forbidden waves,
If Thetis had not, from her deepest caves,
      Restrained their impious thought.

Within the pilgrim's mind what joy was wrought
By this sweet change of amoebean sound!
What wonder, when the hardest rock was found

del néctar numeroso
630   el escollo más duro?
¿Qué mucho, si el candor bebió ya puro
de la virginal copia en la armonía
el veneno del ciego ingenioso
que dictaba los números que oía?

Generosos afectos de una pía
doliente afinidad – bien que amorosa
por bella más, por más divina parte –
solicitan su pecho a que, sin arte
de colores prolijos,
640   en oración impetre oficiosa
del venerable isleño,
que admita yernos los que el trato hijos
litoral hizo, aún antes
que el convecino ardor dulces amantes.

Concediólo risueño,
del forastero agradecidamente
y de sus propios hijos abrazado.
Mercurio destas nuevas diligente,
coronados traslada de favores
650   de sus barcas Amor los pescadores
al flaco pie del suegro deseado.

¡Oh del ave de Júpiter vendado
pollo – si alado, no, lince sin vista –
político rapaz, cuya prudente
disposición especuló estadista
clarísimo ninguno
de los que el reino muran de Neptuno!
¡Cuán dulces te adjudicas ocasiones

A thirsty sponge to drain
The rhythmic nectar's draught!   630
What wonder, when the band of maidens quaffed,
In artless candour, with the harmony,
Venom, which the blind god, who heard the strain
He had inspired, mixed with it cunningly!

The youth was stirred to generous sympathy
For grief so like his own – save that his love
Had sought a fairer, a diviner part –
Which prompted him to try, without the art
    Of highly-coloured speech,
The venerable father's heart to move   640
    To make them sons indeed
Who long since, by the traffic of the beach,
    Had been his kin, before
They came as lovers to the neighbouring shore.

    Smilingly he agreed,
And from the stranger and his family
Received a warm embrace of gratitude.
Love bore the news, an eager Mercury,
And led the fishers, crowned with favours sweet,
Up from their boats to clasp his feeble feet   650
Who now conferred the long-wished fatherhood.

O hoodwinked chick of Jove's imperial brood,
If not a lynx with wings instead of eyes!
Politic youth, whose natural subtlety
No statesman penetrates, however wise,
    Even among their halls
Who fence Poseidon's kingdom with their walls!
How happily you took occasion here

para favorecer, no a dos supremos
660 de los volubles polos ciudadanos,
sino a dos entre cáñamo garzones!
¿Por qué? Por escultores quizá vanos
de tantos de tu madre bultos canos
cuantas al mar espumas dan sus remos.
Al peregrino por tu causa vemos
alcázares dejar, donde, excedida
de la sublimidad la vista, apela
para su hermosura;
en que la arquitectura
670 a la geometría se rebela,
jaspes calzada y pórfidos vestida.
Pobre choza, de redes impedida,
entra ahora, ¡y lo dejas!
¡Vuela, rapaz, y, plumas dando a quejas,
los dos reduce al uno y otro leño,
mientras perdona tu rigor al sueño!

Las horas ya, de números vestidas,
al bayo, cuando no esplendor overo
del luminoso tiro, las pendientes
680 ponían de crisólitos lucientes,
coyundas impedidas,
mientras de su barraca el extranjero
dulcemente salía despedido
a la barquilla, donde le esperaban
a un remo cada joven ofrecido.

Dejaron, pues, las azotadas rocas
que mal las ondas lavan
del livor aún purpúreo de las focas,
y de la firme tierra el heno blando
690 con las palas segando,

To favour, not two deities who dwell
Where round their lofty poles the planets stray,   660
But two poor lads among their fishing gear!
And why? Perhaps, like thriftless sculptors, they
Fashion your mother's shape in silver spray
Each time their oars disperse the hoary swell.
We see the pilgrim, for your sake as well,
Leaving those palaces where, overawed
By height, the eyes must be content to see
    Beauties of door and sill,
    Where architecture's skill
Stands, like a rebel to geometry,   670
Attired in porphyry and in jasper shod.
Now will you leave him on the net-strewn sod
    Of this poor hut, alone?
Fly, boy, and let your feathers mock his moan,
But to their boats at least lead back that pair,
And while they sleep your cruel rigour spare.

Soon as the hours, in numerals arrayed,
Harnessed their shining team of splendid bay
And glowing chestnut steeds and, drawing tight
The bridle-reins of sparkling chrysolite,   680
    Their eager fleetness stayed,
The stranger, sweetly sped upon his way,
Leaving the hut, descended to the shore,
Where the two boys sat in the waiting skiff,
Proffering each the service of an oar.

They leave the beaten coastline where the tide
    But ill can cleanse the cliff
Which with their purple blood the seals have dyed,
Nearing the mainland, till their oar-blades mow
    Its grasses as they row;   690

en la cumbre modesta
de una desigualdad del horizonte,
que deja de ser monte
por ser culta floresta,
antiguo descubrieron blanco muro,
por sus piedras no menos
que por su edad majestuosa cano;
mármol, al fin, tan por lo pario puro,
que al peregrino sus ocultos senos
700   negar pudiera en vano.
Cuantas del océano
el sol trenzas desata
contaba en los rayados capiteles,
que – espejos, aunque esféricos, fieles –
bruñidos eran óvalos de plata.

La admiración que al arte se le debe,
áncora del batel fué, perdonando
poco a lo fuerte, y a lo bello nada
del edificio, cuando
710   ronca los salteó trompa sonante,
al principio distante,
vecina luego, pero siempre incierta.

Llave de la alta puerta
el duro son – vencido el foso breve –
levadiza ofreció puente no leve,
tropa inquieta contra el aire armada,
lisonja, si confusa, regulada
su orden, de la vista, y del oído
su agradable ruido.
720   Verde, no mudo coro
de cazadores era,
cuyo número indigna la ribera.

And where a modest mound,
Seen on the varying skyline, changes from
    A hillside to become
    Fertile and wooded ground,
A white and venerable wall they see,
    Whose very stones attest
Its stately years, in hoary-headed guise,
With Parian marble of such purity
As can withhold no secret of its breast
    From the wayfarer's eyes,   700
    Who, as the sun unties
    His tresses from the sea,
Counts in each shining column's head their splendours
Which every burnished silver oval renders
Back from its convex mirror faithfully.

The admiration which the arts command
Anchors the vessel, and the building's strength
Little, its beauty not at all, they spare
    With gazing, till at length
A trumpet's raucous blast assails their ear,   710
    Distant at first, then near
At hand, though sounding still uncertainly.

    The ancient portal's key
The blast becomes; the narrow moat soon spanned,
The ponderous drawbridge shows a jostling band
Ready in arms for battle with the air,
Whose order, if confused, yet regular,
Flatters the eyesight, while it gratifies
    The hearing with its cries:
    A green but noisy crowd   720
    Of huntsmen, which encumbers
A shore, resentful of their growing numbers.

Al sol levantó apenas la ancha frente
   el veloz hijo ardiente
   del céfiro lascivo
– cuya fecunda madre al genitivo
soplo vistiendo miembros, Guadalete
florida ambrosia al viento dió jinete – ,
   que a mucho humo abriendo
730 la fogosa nariz, en un sonoro
relincho y otro saludó sus rayos.
Los overos, si no esplendores bayos,
   que conducen el día,
les responden, la eclíptica ascendiendo.

Entre el confuso, pues, celoso estruendo
de los caballos, ruda hace armonía,
cuanta la generosa cetrería,
desde la Mauritania a la Noruega,
   insidia ceba alada,
740   sin luz, no siempre ciega,
sin libertad, no siempre aprisionada,
   que a ver el día vuelve
las veces que, en fiado al viento dada,
repite su prisión y al viento absuelve.

El neblí, que, relámpago su pluma,
rayo su garra, su ignorado nido,
o lo esconde el Olimpo o densa es nube
   que pisa, cuando sube
tras la garza argentada el pie de espuma.

750 El sacre, las del noto alas vestido,
sangriento chipriota, aunque nacido
con las palomas, Venus, de tu carro.

Now to the sun their ample brows they lift,
    The offspring bold and swift
    Whom lusty Zephyr sired,
Whose fruitful dam with living limbs attired
The engendering air, while Guadalete feeds
With his ambrosial flowers the wind-born steeds;
    From fiery nostrils wide
They breathe a cloud of smoke, and with a loud   730
Repeated whinny greet the solar rays,
To which the chestnuts and the splendid bays,
    Who mounted steadily
The Zodiac's path with daylight's car, replied.

While steeds in clamorous confusion vied,
Those winged dissemblers made rude harmony,
Whose race is bred by noble falconry
From Moorish desert to Norwegian height.
    Though granted by mankind
    No liberty, no light,   740
They are not always fettered, always blind;
    At times they see the day,
But must, though briefly trusted to the wind,
Regain their prison and their bond repay.

That falcon first, whose wing and claw are fleet
As lightning, and whose nest is none knows where –
Perhaps Olympus or the cloudy height
    Whence he pursues in flight
The silver heron with her foam-flecked feet.

The saker, swift as Auster in the air,   750
Cypriot, athirst for blood, although he share
His nest with birds that draw the car of Love.

El girifalte, escándalo bizarro
del aire, honor robusto de Gelanda,
si bien jayán de cuanto rapaz vuela,
corvo acero su pie, flaca pihuela
de piel lo impide blanda.

El baharí, a quien fué en España cuna
del Pirineo la ceniza verde,
760   o la alta basa que el océano muerde
de la egipcia coluna.

La delicia volante
de cuantos ciñen líbico turbante,
    el borní, cuya ala
en los campos tal vez de Meliona
galán siguió valiente, fatigando
    tímida liebre, cuando
intempestiva salteó leona
    la melionesa gala,
770   que de trágica escena
mucho teatro hizo poca arena.

Tú, infestador, en nuestra Europa nuevo,
de las aves, nacido, aleto, donde
entre las conchas hoy del Sur esconde
    sus muchos años Febo,
    ¿debes por dicha cebo?
¿Templarte supo, dí, bárbara mano
al insultar los aires? Yo lo dudo,
que al preciosamente inca desnudo
780   y al de plumas vestido mejicano,
fraude vulgar, no industria generosa,
del águila les dió a la mariposa.

Then the gerfalcon, stalwart glory of
Zealand, and monstrous wonder of the height,
Though chief of flying robbers, with his strong
Talon of curving steel, a simple thong
    Of leather checks his flight.

Spain makes a cradle for the sparrowhawk
On the green ashes of the Pyrenees,
Or where Gibraltar's pillar feels the seas   760
    Gnawing its base of rock.

    Queen of the feathered kind
For those whose tresses Libyan turbans bind,
    The lanner – who might spy
Below, on Ethiopian plains, some day,
A gallant hunter course a timid hare,
    Eager and unaware,
Then see a lion spring and, now its prey,
    The dusky hero die;
    And for the tragedy   770
But little sand an ample stage would be.

New to our Europe, the destroyer dread
Of other birds, hawk who was born beside
The southern seas where Phoebus now must hide
    His century-laden head,
    For this, then, were you bred?
Could such barbaric hands have made you apt
To affront the air? I must have leave to doubt:
The naked Inca, preciously tricked out,
The savage Mexican in feathers wrapped,   780
By vulgar guile, and not by generous skill,
Alike the butterfly and eagle kill.

De un mancebo serrano
el duro brazo débil hace junco,
examinando con el pico adunco
sus pardas plumas, el azor britano,
tardo, mas generoso
terror de tu sobrino ingenioso,
ya invidia tuya, Dédalo, ave ahora,
790   cuyo pie tiria púrpura colora.

Grave, de perezosas plumas globo,
que a luz lo condenó incierta la ira
del bello de la estigia deidad robo,
desde el guante hasta el hombro a un joven cela:
esta emulación, pues, de cuanto vuela
por dos topacios bellos con que mira,
término torpe era
de pompa tan ligera.

Can, de lanas prolijo, que animoso
800   buzo será, bien de profunda ría,
bien de serena playa,
cuando la fulminada prisión caya
del neblí – a cuyo vuelo,
tan vecino a su cielo,
el Cisne perdonara, luminoso – ,
número y confusión gimiendo hacía
en la vistosa laja para él grave:
que aun de seda no hay vínculo suave.

En sangre claro y en persona augusto,
810   si en miembros no robusto,
príncipe les sucede, abreviada
en modestia civil real grandeza.
La espumosa del Betis ligereza

The British goshawk rode,
With curving beak on dusky plumes intent,
Upon a huntsman's sturdy arm which bent
As though a feeble rush beneath the load,
    Who, slow but generous,
Strikes your ingenious nephew, Daedalus,
With dread – your rival once, now forced to fly,
His foot empurpled in the Tyrian dye.   790

The owl, of sluggish plumes a heavy ball,
Doomed in her anger to uncertain light
By the fair Stygian goddess Pluto stole,
An arm from glove to shoulder occupies.
Envied by every other bird that flies
Those lovely topaz orbs that give him sight,
    He in his dull array
    Bounds the procession gay.

Next, trained to dive, a dog, long-haired and keen
To plumb the river's depth or the profound   800
    Floor of the calmer bay,
And seize the falling thunderbolt of prey
    Dropped by the hawk, who flies
    So near the lofty skies
The shining Swan might let him pass unseen.
Baying, he swells the numbers and the sound,
As on his gaily-coloured leash he strains,
For silken fetters gall no less than chains.

After these came a prince of famous blood,
    Whose noble mien made good   810
Lightness of limb; he seemed a summary
Of civil modesty and regal pride.
His shining steed had drunk from Baethis' tide

bebió no sólo, mas la desatada
majestad en sus ondas, el luciente
caballo que colérico mordía
el oro que suave lo enfrenaba,
arrogante, y no ya por las que daba
estrellas su cerúlea piel al día,
820   sino por lo que siente
de esclarecido y aun de soberano
en la rienda que besa la alta mano,
de cetro digna.

              Lúbrica no tanto
culebra se desliza tortuosa
por el pendiente calvo escollo, cuanto
la escuadra descendía presurosa
por el peinado cerro a la campaña,
que al mar debe con término prescripto
más sabandijas de cristal que a Egipto
830 horrores deja el Nilo que lo baña.

Rebelde ninfa, humilde ahora caña,
    los márgenes oculta
    de una laguna breve,
    a quien doral consulta
    aun el copo más leve
    de su volante nieve.

Ocioso, pues, o de su fin presago,
    los filos con el pico prevenía
    de cuanto sus dos alas aquel día
840 al viento esgrimirán cuchillo vago.

La turba aun no del apacible lago
    las orlas inquieta,

The swiftness of its foam and equally
Shared in its wave's majestic influence.
Impatiently it bit the snaffle-bars
Of gold whose gentle pressure held it in;
Arrogant, not that its cerulean skin
Dappled the morning sky with brighter stars,
    But that it seemed to sense   820
How much nobility and royal command
Lay in the reins that kissed the lofty hand
Worthy a sceptre.

          Never reptile slid
Its smooth and sinuous coils more rapidly
Over some bold and jutting rock than did
Over the furrowed slopes that company,
Descending to the plain with pressing speed,
Which owes the sea, at its appointed bound,
More crystal snakes than are the horrors found
On Egypt's mud when Nilus' waves recede.   830

The rebel nymph, changed to a humble reed,
    Conceals a tiny mere,
    Where a flycatcher now
    Sees in its mirror clear
    To the least flake below
    His whirl of flying snow.

Idly, or else foreseeing his own end,
His quills he sharpens with his beak, that they
May arm his wings against the wind today,
And with their wandering blades his life defend.   840

Before the clamorous multitude descend
    To the calm pool below,

que tímido perdona a sus cristales
el doral. Despedida no saeta
de nervios partos igualar presuma
   sus puntas desiguales,
   que en vano podrá pluma
vestir un leño como viste un ala.

   Puesto en tiempo, corona, si no escala,
850   las nubes – desmintiendo
su libertad el grillo torneado
que en sonoro metal lo va siguiendo –
   un baharí templado,
   a quien el mismo escollo
– a pesar de sus pinos, eminente –
el primer vello le concedió pollo,
que al Betis las primeras ondas fuente.

   No sólo, no, del pájaro pendiente,
las caladas registra el peregrino,
860   mas del terreno cuenta cristalino
   los juncos más pequeños,
verdes hilos de aljófares risueños.

   Rápido al español alado mira
peinar el aire por cardar el vuelo,
cuya vestida nieve anima un hielo
que torpe a unos carrizos lo retira,
   infieles por raros,
   si firmes no por trémulos reparos.

   Penetra, pues, sus inconstantes senos,
870   estimándolos menos
   entredichos que el viento;
mas a su daño el escuadrón atento,

The bird forsakes its crystal glass in fright.
Never could shaft discharged from Parthian bow
The speed of these unequal wings presume
    To equal in its flight,
    Because no borrowed plume
Can dress an arrow as a wing is dressed.

A sparrowhawk, seasonably released,
    Hungry for quarry, crowned   850
Rather than scaled the clouds, though tethered by
A bell, whose metal clasp and ceaseless sound
    His liberty belie.
    The selfsame mountainside,
Lofty despite its pine-trees, which conferred
Upon Guadalquivir its infant tide,
Clothed with its earliest down the fledgling bird.

The pilgrim's eye not only registered
The hovering falcon's spirals, but his glance
Counted upon the crystalline expanse   860
    The tiniest reeds, among
Whose threads of verdure smiling pearls were hung.

The fleet-winged Spanish hawk he now descried
Which combed the air to card the other's flight,
Who felt his snowy vesture freeze with fright
And sought, faint-hearted, in the reeds to hide –
    Treacherous because so few,
And insecure, because so feeble too.

He plunged within their fickle bosom where
    Safer than in the air   870
    He seemed, but soon the rout,
Intent upon his ruin, drove him out,

expulso lo remite a quien en suma
un grillo y otro enmudeció en su pluma.

Cobrado el baharí, en su propio luto,
o el insulto acusaba precedente,
    o entre la verde hierba
    avara escondía cuerva
purpúreo caracol, émulo bruto
880   del rubí más ardiente,
cuando, solicitada del ruido,
el nácar a las flores fía torcido,
y con siniestra voz convoca cuanta
    negra de cuervas suma
infamó la verdura con su pluma,
con su número el sol. En sombra tanta
alas desplegó Ascálafo prolijas,
    verde poso ocupando,
    que de césped ya blando,
890 jaspe lo han hecho duro blancas guijas.

Más tardó en desplegar sus plumas graves
el deforme fiscal de Proserpina,
que en desatarse, al polo ya vecina,
la disonante niebla de las aves;
diez a diez se calaron, ciento a ciento,
al oro intuitivo, invidiado
    deste género alado,
si como ingrato no, como avariento,
que a las estrellas hoy del firmamento
900   se atreviera su vuelo
    en cuanto ojos del cielo.

Poca palestra la región vacía,
    de tanta invidia era,

To one who in his wings, with talons fell,
Buried his jesses, silencing his bell.

The hawk recaptured, with black wings there came,
As though he mourned the late affront, a crow,
    Or else perhaps he tried
    Among the grass to hide
A purple snail which, though an uncut gem,
    Rivalled the ruby's glow.   880
Attracted by the huntsmen's din, confiding
The twisted nacre to the flowers for hiding,
He summoned every crow with grating call,
    And soon their black array
Soiled with their wings the green and hid the day
By force of numbers. Darkness seemed to fall,
And, opening monstrous vans, Ascalaphus
    Flew to a mound of green
    Where pebbles, white of sheen,
Like jasper turned to stone the tender grass.   890

Persephone's grotesque accuser spread
His ponderous wings so slowly, he allowed
The birds, who now detached their raucous cloud
From the high pole, to swoop upon his head.
By tens and hundreds, with tumultuous speed,
They sought the imagined gold, the dear desire
    Of all their feathered choir,
Yet not so much in malice as in greed,
For they had soared aloft today indeed
    Only because the skies   900
    Have stars that shine like eyes.

Too small arena could the empty blue
    For so much greed afford,

mientras, desenlazado la cimera,
    restituyen el día
a un girifalte, boreal arpía,
que, despreciando la mentida nube,
    a luz más cierta sube,
cenit ya de la turba fugitiva.

910   Auxiliar taladra el aire luego
un duro sacre, en globos no de fuego,
    en oblicuos sí engaños
mintiendo remisión a las que huyen,
    si la distancia es mucha:
griego al fin. Una en tanto, que de arriba
descendió fulminada en poco humo,
apenas el latón segundo escucha,
que del inferior peligro al sumo
apela, entre los trópicos grifaños
920   que su eclíptica incluyen,
    repitiendo confusa
    lo que tímida excusa.

    Breve esfera de viento,
negra circunvestida piel, al duro
alterno impulso de valientes palas,
    la avecilla parece,
en el de muros líquidos que ofrece
corredor el diáfano elemento
al gémino rigor, en cuyas alas
930   su vista libra toda el extranjero.

    Tirano el sacre de lo menos puro
desta primer región, sañudo espera
la desplumada ya, la breve esfera,

But now the hood was lifted which restored
    To a gerfalcon's view
The light of day, a boreal harpy who,
Scorning the specious cloud, in loftier flight
    To find a surer light,
Became the zenith of the elusive flock.

Now to his aid a sturdy saker came   910
Who drilled the air, though not with balls of flame,
    Crooked and sly he was,
And pardon to the flying foe he feigned,
    Judging his distance well,
A Greek for guile. Then like a puff of smoke
Fell from above, as thunderstruck, a crow,
Who had no sooner heard the other's bell
Than from the threat above to that below
He swerved, as if the tropics of their claws
    His zodiac contained,   920
    Seeking, confused, once more
    The ill he shunned before.

    Brief plaything of the wind
The little bird appeared, now to and fro,
Black skin-clad ball, by cruel buffetings
    From two hard raquets sent,
Offered by the transparent element
A court, by only liquid walls confined,
For the twin rigour of the hawks, whose wings
Alone the stranger fixed with eager look.   930

Tyrant of the impurer lower air,
The saker waited spitefully until
The tiny sphere, now stripped of every quill,

que, a un bote corvo del fatal acero,
dejó al viento, si no restituído,
heredado en el último graznido.

Destos pendientes agradables casos
vencida se apeó la vista apenas,
que del batel, cosido con la playa,
940   cuantos da la cansada turba pasos,
    tantos en las arenas
el remo perezosamente raya,
a la solicitud de una atalaya
atento, a quien doctrina ya cetrera
    llamó catarribera.

Ruda en esto política, agregados
tan mal ofrece como construídos
bucólicos albergues, si no flacas
    piscatorias barracas,
950   que pacen campos, que penetran senos,
    de las ondas no menos
    aquéllos perdonados
que de la tierra éstos admitidos.

Pollos, si de las propias no vestidos,
de las maternas plumas abrigados,
vecinos eran destas alquerías,
mientras ocupan a sus naturales,
Glauco en las aguas, y en las hierbas Pales.

¡Oh cuántas cometer piraterías
960   un cosario intentó y otro volante
– uno y otro rapaz digo milano –,
    bien que todas en vano,
contra la infantería, que piante

Struck by the steel that armed the fatal hook,
Left to the wind, bequeathed if not restored,
The heritage his dying caws afford.

From these fair pendant sights when they had ceased
To gaze, their eyes defeated, from the boat
Which followed, as if stitched, the winding shore,
As many steps the weary huntsmen paced,   940
    So many times they smote
The underlying sand with sluggish oar,
Attentive to his vigilance, who bore
The name 'catarribera', if we choose
    The term that falconers use.

Located here by rustic policy
Dwellings, as ill contrived as badly planned,
Had risen, wretched piscatorial huts,
    If not bucolic cots;
They grazed upon the meadows and caressed   950
    The encroaching ocean's breast,
    Those pardoned by the sea
No less than these were suffered by the land.

Chickens who, lacking their own feathers, found
Beneath their mother's wings a sanctuary,
Were the near neighbours of these cottages,
Whose tenants followed Glaucus on the sea
Or honoured Pales with their husbandry.

Intent upon how many piracies
Was one and other flying privateer   960
– Both kites, I warrant, of rapacious strain –
    But they attacked in vain
This infantry which, chirruping with fear,

en su madre se esconde, donde halla
voz que es trompeta, pluma que es muralla.

A media rienda en tanto el anhelante
caballo – que el ardiente sudor niega
en cuantas le densó nieblas su aliento –
a los indignos de ser muros llega
970   céspedes, de las ovas mal atados.

Aunque ociosos, no menos fatigados,
quejándose venían sobre el guante
los raudos torbellinos de Noruega.
Con sordo luego estrépito despliega
– injuria de la luz, horror del viento –
sus alas el testigo que en prolija
desconfianza a la sicana diosa
      dejó sin dulce hija,
y a la estigia deidad con bella esposa.

Sheltered beneath their mother, while she made
Her voice their trump, her plumes their barricade.

Next, at half rein, the panting horse, who strove
To hide, with breath that cooled in clouds of steam,
The sweat that on his glowing body lay,
Came to these dwellings, worthy scarce the name,
Whose turf and seaweed bound their walls but ill.   970

Not less fatigued, though even more sluggish still,
Each perched, complaining loudly, on his glove,
The swift Norwegian whirlwinds slowly passed.
Then with a muffled crash of sound at last –
Bane of the air and outrage of the day –
He spread his wings, whose testimony left
Sicania's goddess long disconsolate,
    Of her sweet child bereft
To give the Stygian king a lovely mate.

APPENDIX

Góngora made various alterations to the text of the *Sole-dades* in the course of successive editions. The Spanish printed in the preceding pages represents the final form, but admirers of the poem have often expressed regret at the changes made to lines 197-211 of the First Solitude which, we are told, were revised on the advice of Pedro de Valencia. The earlier text ran as follows:

Muda la admiración, habla callando,
y, ciega, un río sigue, que – luciente
        de aquellos montes hijo –
con torcido discurso, si prolijo,
tiraniza los campos útilmente;
orladas sus orillas de frutales,
si de flores, tomadas, no, a la broca,
derecho corre mientras no revoca
los mismos autos el de sus cristales;
huye un trecho de sí, alcánzase luego;
desvíase, y, buscando sus desvíos,
errores dulces, dulces desvaríos
hacen sus aguas con lascivo juego;
engazando edificios en su plata,
de quintas coronado, se dilata
        majestuosamente
– en brazos dividido caudalosos
de islas, que paréntesis frondosos
al período son de su corriente –
de la alta gruta donde se desata

hasta los jaspes líquidos, adonde
su orgullo pierde y su memoria esconde.

The following is an attempt to render the passage in English:

Wonder, though mute, in silence speaks; though blind
Follows the shining stream, which had its birth
Among those heights, whose course,
Tortuous at once and prolix, can enforce
Tyrannous abundance on the neighbouring earth.
A fringe of orchards on its banks is spread
And flowers embroidered by no needle's stroke.
First running straight, then seeming to revoke
The very edicts that its crystals made,
It seems to flee itself, then doubling back,
It loses and regains its devious way
And, erring sweetly, sweetly goes astray,
Winding its ripples on a wanton track.
Houses are linked along its silver tide
And goodly manors, as its waters glide
Majestically broad,
Now branching into arms, in whose embrace
Islands are clasped, leafy parentheses
To interrupt its current's period,
From the high cavern whence it was untied,
Till in the liquid jasper of the sea
It sinks its pride and veils its memory.

Date Due